ALL THE TORS

E P Woodhouse

ALL THE TORS

E P Woodhouse

First published in Great Britain in 2020
by TRAVELLING LINES PRESS

This book is a work of non-fiction based on the life, experiences and recollections of E P Woodhouse. In some limited cases the names of people, places, dates and sequences or the detail of events have been changed to protect the privacy of others.

Every effort has been made to obtain the necessary permissions with reference to copyright material. We apologise for any omissions in this respect and will be pleased to make the appropriate acknowledgments or rectify any perceived errors in any future edition.

ISBN 978-1-9160341-1-2 (Hardback)
ISBN 978-1-9160341-2-9 (E-book)

10 9 8 7 6 5 4 3 2 1

To Dartmoor,
the love of my life.

CONTENTS

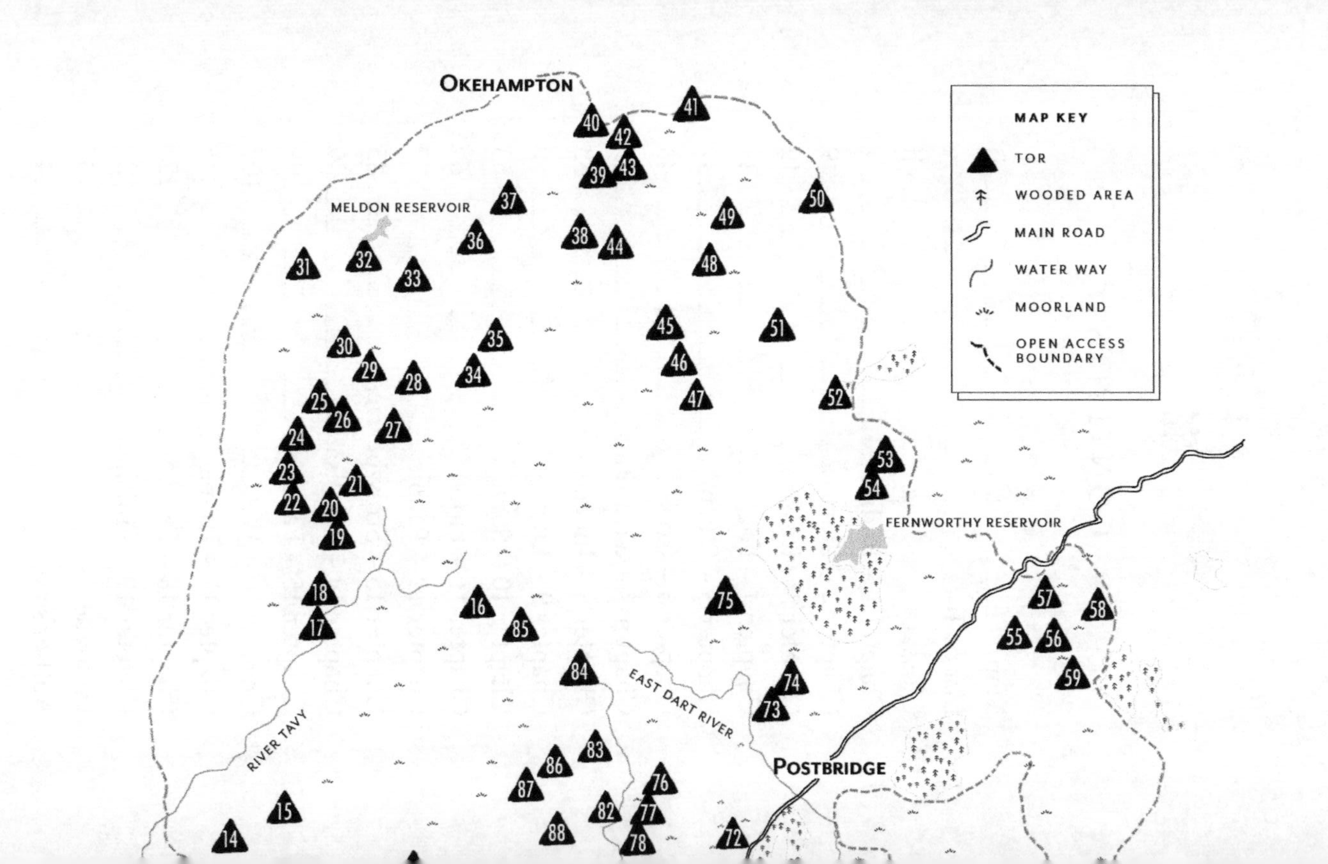
OKEHAMPTON
MELDON RESERVOIR
FERNWORTHY RESERVOIR
EAST DART RIVER
RIVER TAVY
POSTBRIDGE
MAP KEY
TOR
WOODED AREA
MAIN ROAD
WATER WAY
MOORLAND
OPEN ACCESS BOUNDARY
14
15
16
17
18
19
20
21
22
23
24
25
26
27
28
29
30
31
32
33
34
35
36
37
38
39
40
41
42
43
44
45
46
47
48
49
50
51
52
53
54
55
56
57
58
59
72
73
74
75
76
77
78
82
83
84
85
86
87
88

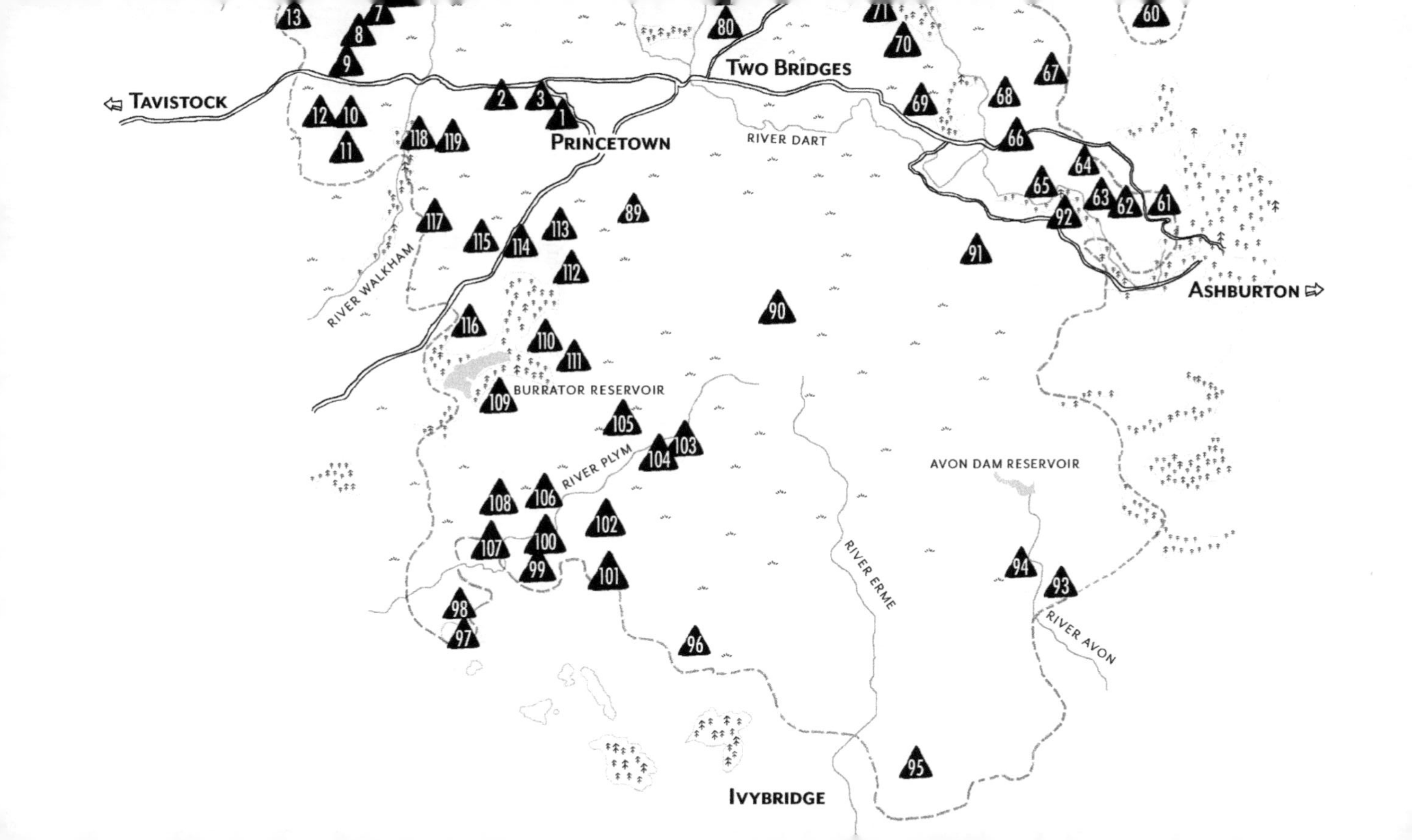
Tavistock
Two Bridges
Princetown
River Dart
River Walkham
Burrator Reservoir
River Plym
Ashburton
Avon Dam Reservoir
River Erme
River Avon
Ivybridge
13
7
8
9
12
10
11
118
119
2
3
1
80
71
70
69
68
67
66
65
64
63
62
61
60
92
91
117
115
114
113
112
89
90
116
110
111
109
105
104
103
108
106
102
107
100
99
101
98
97
96
94
93
95

THE LIST OF TORS

1 North Hessary
2 Hollow
3 Rundlestone
4 Little Mis
5 Great Mis
6 Roos
7 Great Staple
8 Middle Staple
9 Little Staple
10 Heckwood
11 Pew
12 Feather
13 Cox
14 Boulters
15 White
16 Lynch
17 Nat
18 Ger
19 Hare
20 Sharp
21 Chat
22 Doe
23 Brat
24 Arms
25 Little Links
26 Great Links
27 Green
28 Kitty
29 Hunt
30 Gren
31 Sourton
32 Shelstone
33 Black
34 Lints
35 Dinger
36 Yes
37 West Mill
38 East Mill
39 Winter
40 Scarey
41 Ivy
42 Belstone
43 Higher
44 Oke
45 Steeperton
46 Wild
47 Watern
48 Hound
49 Little Hound
50 Shilstone
51 Rival
52 Scorhill
53 Middle
54 Thornworthy

55 Birch
56 Hookney
57 Shapley
58 King
59 Hameldown
60 Wind
61 Leigh
62 Aish
63 Hockingston
64 Mel
65 Luckey
66 Sharp
67 Corndon
68 Yar
69 Huccaby
70 Laughter
71 Bellever
72 Arch
73 Hartland
74 Stannon
75 Sittaford
76 Lower White
77 Higher White
78 Longaford
79 Littaford
80 Crockern
81 Beardown
82 Crow
83 Rough
84 Flat
85 Fur
86 Devil's
87 Conies Down
88 Lydford
89 South Hessary
90 Fox
91 Combestone
92 Bench
93 Shipley
94 Black
95 Sharp
96 Rook
97 Collard
98 Hawk's
99 Little Trowlesworthy
100 Great Trowlesworthy
101 Hen
102 Shavercombe
103 Calverslake
104 Lower Hartor
105 Higher Hartor
106 Eastern
107 Legis
108 Gutter
109 Sheeps
110 Down
111 Combeshead
112 Cramber
113 Hart
114 Black
115 Leeden
116 Leather
117 Ingra
118 Hucken
119 King's

GLOSSARY

Tor *(Cornu-Celtic, twr, tower)*: a granite outcrop, usually on the top or side of a hill. Often appearing as a towering stack of rock. The word is often used to refer to the hill itself, with the rock marking the summit.

Leat *(Old English, wætergelæt, water channel)*: a narrow man-made waterway, with straight banks, often flowing imperceptibly slowly around a hill.

Clitter *(Celtic, clegyr, rock)*: a boulder field of granite blocks, each at least the size of a large loaf of bread. Typically this is the ancient eroded debris from a tor, strewn across the hillside below it.

DofE: contraction of 'Duke of Edinburgh's Award'. A youth awards programme at three levels: Bronze, Silver and Gold. Participants must complete the four main sections of volunteering, skills, physical and an expedition.

Range Poles: red and white striped metal poles that mark the boundary of a military range. They are placed upright in the ground and spaced 100 metres or so apart.

Letterbox: a small container with a stamp, ink pad and visitor's book inside. They are hidden across Dartmoor to be found like a treasure hunt. Those who have visited 100 boxes, stamping their own booklet for proof, may join the 100 Club. 'Letterboxing' was invented by the Victorians.

GLOSSARY

CHAPTER 1 – RADIO

All I wanted was to stay in bed as long as practically possible. It's the perfect way to minimise expedition morning nerves. You can't be nervous if you're not awake. Instead, I sat on the floor of my parents' bedroom, purple jumper pulled on over red pyjamas, staring across the room at our landline phone. Waiting.

I'd wanted to get up even earlier to prepare, but there was only so far I'd go. They'd already put me in a slot a good hour earlier than I'd normally get out of bed. Talking is not something that I list among my strengths. Neither is making lucid conversation before 9 am. Early mornings and I only mix well in tents.

As I stared at the phone, I thought through all of the reasons why I shouldn't have accepted an invitation to be interviewed on the radio. I tried to shake my head out of its early morning daze. Why did I have to make life difficult for myself? Was today not hard enough already? The longer I sat in silence with the phone, the more the dread grew.

Of course, I knew exactly why I'd agreed. Alongside my challenge, I was raising funds for Dartmoor Rescue. At the time I'd been pleased to accept, grateful to be offered a spot on the show. But the Emily who'd rolled out of bed half an hour beforehand was having serious doubts.

The phone rang. It's blaring staccato noise jarring the silence, making me start. I leant over and picked up the receiver, stretching its spiral cable between the wall and my ear. A lady's voice ran me through what was going to happen while we stood by for the allocated time. Then silence. I waited. They put me on.

Aside from exhaustion and regret, I also had very low expectations. My only prior experience of radio interviews was being stood up for one. It had taken a couple of weeks to organise. I'd spent the whole afternoon before being nervous about it until they'd finally rung me, at the planned time, to say another guest had overrun. I was being cut. It seemed that being on the list was nothing special and it was never rearranged.

Low as my expectations were, I did imagine that they might ask me a few questions about the challenge I was about to set off on. You know, the reason they wanted me on their show in the first place. Instead we bumbled through tangential subjects, including the meaning behind the motto in my email signature. By the end of the 15 minutes my puzzled morning head was dazed and embarrassed. Had I missed something? I was left feeling like I'd showed up to a party in fancy dress, while everyone else was wearing fancy dresses.

As my section ended, the lady's voice came back onto the phone, "Emily, before you go, you might just want to stay on the line a minute and listen to the weather forecast. It'll be coming on the radio in a moment."

"No thank you," I said cheerily, seething. "I know what the weather's going to be doing, thanks!"

Funnily enough, I had checked the forecast.

"Well there's this big storm coming through and you might want to..."

Might want to what? Put off the walk? Tell everyone I'm leaving and then not go?

"Yes, thank you," I said, "I've seen the forecast. Thanks very much though."

"Okay, well if you're sure..."

"Yep, thanks very much though... Okay. Bye now. Bye."

I put the phone down. Foggy. It was foggy. What they didn't know from their studio in Plymouth was I could see that out the window.

Downstairs in the kitchen, my parents were sitting at the table having breakfast.

"How did it go?" asked Mum as I entered.

"Ach, fine," I said, pouring my cereal and sitting down with a thump. "They didn't give me a chance to share my fundraising link and asked me really weird questions... We barely talked about the challenge."

"Ah well, never mind."

I'd picked up the phone ready to talk about how I was

feeling, my planning process and why I was doing it in the first place. You know what they say: fail to prepare and prepare to make a public embarrassment of yourself on live air. Not that that had helped. This was the boldest challenge of my life, although perhaps not the biggest. Why hadn't they asked me about it?

"There's still plenty of time for people to find out about it," said Mum. "I'm sure you'll get another chance."

"Yeah, I suppose."

I looked across at my rucksack, propped against the kitchen wall. It was, almost literally, the elephant in the room: a grey, 60 litre monster of a bag. I'd stuffed it to the brim with clothes, camping equipment and food. The years of hand-sewn repairs and strategically placed rucksack patches only adding to its appearance of exploding at the seams. You had to carry a lot of food for 10 days. But it was just 10 days. Ten days and a huge rucksack on Dartmoor. I knew all about carrying huge backpacks on Dartmoor.

I turned my attention back to my cereal.

"It's a little foggy out," said Mum, quietly.

Before long, it was time to leave. I laced up my leather walking boots and zipped up my gaiters. Sitting down next to my rucksack, I shuffled between the straps, did up all the clips and hauled myself back upright. It felt as though Dad was watching me closely as I put it on.

"Ready!" I exclaimed.

Mum gave me a nervous smile.

"Would you like me to carry the bag out to the car for you?" asked Dad.

"Err, no it's alright," I said. "I'm going to have to carry it for the next 10 days – I may as well get started now."

I put my hands on my hips and grinned as if it was the easiest thing in the world.

"No need to carry it unnecessarily."

Last night he'd given me quite a stern talking to about not breaking myself on this expedition. It was my mistake, really. I'd left the bag in the kitchen, ready for the morning. He'd tried to pick it up. It was very heavy.

The original plan had been to collect food packages along the way. But that seemed like a logistical nightmare and anyway, I thought I could carry it all. So many people had told me I couldn't that I just had to try – and lo and behold, it fitted. Just.

"There's no shame in accepting help," he'd said. "If you find you can't carry it, just call us. We'll come and take some things off you, then drive back out with it later on. There's no glory in giving yourself an injury."

Rucksack strapped into the car, we drove to Princetown. The closer we got, the thicker the mist became. Beneath it, the grass was starting to lose its green, dulling towards the browns and ochres of autumn. I looked out of the window dismally. We often get low cloud in the mornings, I told myself. It'll clear. It'll clear.

"It's very foggy," said Mum eventually. "Are you sure you'll be alright?"

"Yes," I sighed, "I've had to navigate in worse weather than this. It's rarely ever sunny when we get called out for

Dartmoor Rescue. And anyway, there's no other start date that'll work with the firing times... and I've booked time off work. It has to be now."

"I hope the weather clears up for you."

"Me too... but even if it doesn't, I've got all the skills I need from Ten Tors and Dartmoor Rescue and leading groups and everything."

The Ten Tors Challenge is a walking event, organised by the Army, that takes places on Dartmoor once a year. Local teenagers train for months to be able to lug their backpacks around 35, 45 or 55 miles – camping out in the middle of the moor overnight. The alphabet of routes take in a big loop of Dartmoor, from north to south and back again.

Ten Tors is something of an institution in Devon, to the extent that you can reasonably start to identify by your mileage: I'm a 35, next year I'll be a 45, maybe I'll do 55 one day. Always a glutton for punishment, I did the challenge four years in a row at different mileages. My team even beat a couple of speed records. Now I was a volunteer leader for the same walking group I'd done it through: the Dartmoor Plodders.

"Plus," I continued, still on the defensive, "I've got a GPS tracker so you'll be able to see exactly where I am all the time."

This didn't convince Mum. "I wish someone else was going with you..."

I sighed again, gazing out the window at the swirling mist,"Yeah, well, who exactly would sign up for something like this?" I stopped, realising I was making the trip sound extra hard and quickly added, "And anyway, all my friends have got someone more important to spend their annual leave on." I paused. I was digging a different hole. "Not in a bad way... but, you know, like they need to spend time with their family – or they've got work or kids or something..." I looked back out of the window, "This is just between me and Dartmoor."

CHAPTER 2 – START

Princetown town centre was a hive of activity. There were troops of families, decked out in waterproofs, unpacking rucksacks from their cars. Outside the grand columned front of Dartmoor National Park Visitor Centre, the square was teeming with people. Everyone was dressed for the outdoors. None of them were here for me. It was all just an unfortunate timetabling clash.

This morning was the start of Dartmoor Rescue Team's 11 Tors Challenge, an event I was supposed to be helping organise. Despite its grandiose name, it's only a short day walk: 11 tors over 11 miles. I'd suggested it as a joke in the planning meeting, a cheeky one-up on Ten Tors. It had stuck. Now here I was taking the sentiment to the extreme.

I'd intended to have a specific launch event. That's what adventurers do, isn't it? I had my route and timescales all mapped out. But everything depended on when I could get into each of the ranges. When the live firing times for the three Dartmoor ranges were finally released, six weeks in advance, I realised I had a problem. Without completely reshaping my route or waiting another month, there was only one pattern of day and night firing that would allow me to pass through safely. That left me starting in Princetown on 11 Tors Saturday.

The bright red Dartmoor Rescue gazebo was set up in the middle of the square. I walked over to see how I could help. In Dartmoor Rescue, everything is red. It starts with the team-issued red jackets, emblazoned with Mountain Rescue, but it doesn't stop there. Before you know it you're subconsciously buying a wardrobe full of red clothing and saving up for an off-road vehicle. I'd been in the Team for three years now and somehow I was still the youngest.

The crowd in the square slowly shifted. Apparently, this disordered mass of people was three separate queues for 11 Tors team registration. Split into thirds alphabetically by team, some people were having a hard time remembering which witty name they'd put on their booking form. I ducked under the awning, behind the desk.

"Hey, I'm here – can I help with anything?"

I'd been dealing with all the bookings before the event. Surely they could use my help somehow; registration was well underway. Someone glanced backwards over their shoulder, hands still working at the desk.

"No, er, we're fine thanks. Got it covered."

"Oh. Okay then."

I got back out of their way, wondering what to do with

myself. My parents appeared and Dad handed me the car keys.

"So you can get your rucksack out when you want it," he said. "We'll be over in the square."

"Thanks. Oh, well I guess I may as well get it now."

On the way back over to the car, I bumped into the Dartmoor Plodders, a small group of people in luminous green t-shirts. We'd worn blue t-shirts once, when I was about 16, but they just didn't stand out enough. Since then the green has been getting more lurid every year.

How to begin to explain the Dartmoor Plodders? On the face of it, I suppose you'd say it's a walking group that fields Ten Tors teams every year. It's not the only event we enter but it's certainly the biggest. We're an independent group, so take teenagers from any school and pretty much anywhere, as long as they can make the training walks.

But the Plodders is much more than that. It's not just another bland Ten Tors team churning kids through the system each year. It's a mindset, an attitude, a decision to step off the normal path and do things differently. The Plodders is all about quirky traditions, mantras, passing on legends and an illustrious history of winning things. Our teams don't always beat records, but it takes the level of a leg amputation for someone to be dropped out of a walking event. That's all part of the motto: No Retreat No Surrender.

The Plodders has shaped about a decade of my life. Like many, I joined because I'd fallen through the cracks in another team. But I stayed because I loved it. There was a wildness and freedom to it that school teams simply wouldn't allow. Plus a sense of being part of something bigger, older and wackier than yourself – an unusual set of people following an unusual set of rules. After university, I came back as a leader and in many ways it was like I'd never left. They say some people never really do. I was more than happy to carry on the grand tradition and help put a new spin on what, as a teenager, the leaders had done for me.

In the car park two other leaders, Huck and Laura, were assembling a group of young people and parents, here to walk the 11 Tors Challenge. All three of us had done Ten Tors with the Plodders and stuck around as we got older. Huck was doing 45 while I was doing 55. Laura had come through the ranks while I was away at university.

One of the teenagers came up to me.

"Are you really going to walk to all the tors? Huck told me," he added quickly.

"Yes I am."

"How many are there?"

"One hundred and nineteen."

"Woah."

I smiled, trying to keep up the persona of a competent adult whilst freaking out inside. It did sound impressive. Huck herded them all in the direction of the registration table.

"How are you feeling?" asked Laura, staying behind as I got my bag.

"Like a 35 staring down the start line of the event..." I admitted.

I used to hate that bit: the waiting. At the start of the Ten Tors event, every year, teams assemble on the hill above

Okehampton Army Camp. In a crowd of 2000 people, you stand in silence, one tiny person facing out towards the whole of Dartmoor. The enormity of what you are about to do slowly sinking in.

Down below, hidden by the crowd, some people would be talking into a microphone, introducing the event. But all that reaches the hillside is a monotone mumble. So you just wait, heart in stomach, bracing, waiting for the start and the stampede down the hill. A whole year's worth of training and suffering had led up to this moment. Every miserable camp, every blister – everything you'd done to get a place on the start line. This was your chance to make it count and you got one shot.

Except this time I hadn't done any training. The All the Tors Challenge would be the longest, furthest continuous walk I had ever done and I hadn't trained – at least nothing especially. Nothing above the ordinary time I spent on the moor with the Plodders and Dartmoor Rescue. I felt like I should have done something special to prepare myself, some sort of fitness regime or extra practice.

"Why are you nervous?" asked Laura, as we crossed the car park back towards the crowds. "This is your thing."

I hauled my bag over from the boot of the car into the back of the gazebo. Outside the Visitor Centre, the square was still busy although the initial surge of teams had set off. It was easy to spot my parents: two people standing anxiously and silent in a crowd of people excited about a fun day's walk. I went to them.

As we stood waiting, Mike from Dartmoor National

Park Authority stepped out of their building. In the run up to the expedition, I'd been working with the National Park as an ambassador. We were hoping to use my walk to promote responsible wild camping. Mike was my main point of contact and he'd come to wish me well. He joined our stationary bubble while people in red jackets rushed past us in all directions. Handheld radios chattered in the background: the first few teams had reached the first checkpoint.

"I was having a look over your route last night," said Mike. "Looks like you'll have a good one."

I had a sinking moment of realisation. I'd given a copy of my route to the Team and to Dartmoor National Park. I'd made sure every one of my social media followers had access to my tracking map. I'd kept my blog and friends updated… but not my parents. Fifteen minutes until the start and I realised they might like to know where I was going.

"What route card is this…?" asked Mum.

At that moment, Andy happened to be walking past. He was the Team's Secretary and, being the Treasurer myself, we spent a fair bit of time together. Everyone in the Team has an interesting backstory. We are a remarkably eclectic group of people, made uniform by a love of Dartmoor and the colour red. Andy had, amongst other things, holy orders and project management in his backstory – which made him easy to talk to and great at organising things.

"Hey Andy!" I called. He stopped. "I don't suppose you could send that spreadsheet with my route card on to my parents? They have the tracker link, but not where I'm actually aiming to camp and all that."

I hadn't thought it would be important. He raised his eyebrow ever so slightly – really Emily?

"It's on my laptop at home," I continued, "but they won't be able to find it now."

"Sure," he grinned wryly, turning to my parents. "What's your email address?"

Just then, a photographer for the local paper arrived and I was pulled away for photos. I strained a smile and felt strangely absent as they posed me, wearing a Dartmoor Rescue t-shirt and my enormous rucksack. I thought of my collection of group photos from the morning of each Ten Tors event. Everyone looking cold and miserable, bleary-eyed from waking up at 4:30 am to beat the queue for the porter loos. Trying to find the delicate balance between smiles, nerves and keeping down that bacon sandwich you'd been forced to finish.

Eventually, the photographer was pleased with what he'd got. I put the bag back down and walked away.

After pre-event photos, on the morning of Ten Tors, you'd join the long solemn procession up through the Camp and out onto the moors at Anthony's Stile. If you're a Dartmoor Plodder, you get there early and turn aside from the crowd for last minute preparations. The leaders organise a warm up. A helicopter swings by to deliver a field gun to the bottom of the hill – or the cannon as we used to call it. You need a pretty loud bang for the Ten Tors starting pistol.

Warm up completed Stu, the Plodders' team manager,

would give us some wise words of confidence, a handshake, a pat on the shoulder, a hug maybe for the tearful. It was a shame he couldn't be here today. Then, all goodbyes said and luck given, you'd find your route letter, walk to the front of the queue and wait. It always ended in the same way: waiting for the gun to fire and the moment when the whole hillside lurches forward as one. Eager to be off. Running, pushed from behind down into the bog before fanning out in all directions.

Where was my starting gun now? I just wanted the wait to be over with. I just wanted to be gone, to start. Once it started it was just another walk. The square was almost empty now. It was just me and my parents and a few people in red dotted around. I realised I was still sitting there waiting for the sign to start – waiting for that cannon. But there wasn't going to be one.

"Well, um, I'm going to go now then," I announced to no one in particular.

I said a final goodbye to my parents and started to slowly drift away, as if sneaking out the back exit of building.

"Bye then…"

This was weird. Please, someone fire the gun!

"Oh, are you off?" A few people started to notice. "See you then…"

Andy whipped out his phone and started to record me leaving. I edged away, turning and waving behind me as I went.

"Okay, well see you then. Bye, bye..."

I got past the gazebo. As soon as I was blocked from

view, I turned and headed straight out of Princetown as fast as I could. If I could have run with my rucksack on, I probably would have sprinted.

CHAPTER 3 – REASONS

Twenty minutes later, I stood on top of North Hessary Tor. It had started: tor number one. The morning mist was dissipating into wispy clumps of thin cloud. I breathed a massive sigh of relief, standing in the fresh Dartmoor breeze. It had begun. This crazy idea was finally happening. I had taken my first step towards walking all the tors on Dartmoor in one continuous circuit: 300 kilometres over 10 days, solo and carrying everything I needed on my back.

North Hessary Tor was a checkpoint for the 11 Tors Challenge. Between the tor and the TV mast was a small group of Team members, with red jackets and clip boards.

"Hear you're off on a big walk," they said, as if it was just another one of Emily's crazy ideas. Which, in fairness, I suppose it was. This was the girl who'd missed her first navigation assessment because she hadn't cycled back from

Switzerland fast enough.

"Yeah, that's right."

I hadn't really made a big deal about it with the Team. Most of them knew I was doing something, some big walk, but none of the detail. They certainly didn't know how much it meant to me. Everyone had been asked to do some fundraising as part of the 50th celebrations. I guess this was sort of mine.

It was Dartmoor Rescue's 50th anniversary this year and, as it turned out, my 25th year on the planet. Such an alignment of numbers had seemed somehow momentous – like an opportunity to do something special, something I'd been curious about for years.

Ever since I'd finished Ten Tors, there had been an innocuous little question lurking in the back of my mind: I wonder if you can do all of them? Not even me specifically, but whether it was physically possible. How many were there? How far would it be? At the end of 55, clutching a shiny gold medal and a cheap pasty, you're left wondering what's next. Ten Tors had been very achievable and it doesn't take a vast leap of imagination to get from 10 to every single one.

"So tell me Emily, how many tors are you doing?"

"All the tors: one hundred and nineteen."

"There are more tors on Dartmoor than that."

I rolled my eyes and put on my best Terms and Conditions voice, "All the tors marked on OL 28 as 'Something' space 'Tor' within the connected component of Open Access Land."

Not as catchy, but the precise definition. I was calling

it my Disclaimer for Dartmoor Nerds. To everyone else, I was doing all the tors marked on the most common map of Dartmoor that I could legally access in one round trip. That didn't sound so unreasonable, but people can be picky.

I left North Hessary Tor and headed away from Princetown, cutting in and out of the 11 Tors routes as I collected my tors. The grass was crispy and dry underfoot, still green but showing the tell-tale signs of the changing season. The tors this side of Princetown were small and numerous, friendly and distinctive lumps of granite topping every one.

We used to come to here a lot when we first moved to Dartmoor. It was close to home and fairly tame, with lots of rocks and holes and leats and bridges for small children to explore. A wild extension of a back garden. I was almost at the end of primary school when we moved here, not yet in double digits. Coming from the bland South East of England, I found the bleak landscape of Dartmoor fascinating.

There is a local word for people like me: grockle. It means an outsider, a visitor to Devon, someone who doesn't quite fit in with the way things work down here. It's not a rude or offensive word, something you might say in jest or accompanied by tut and a cheeky flick of the eyes, "All those grockles in their campervans blocking up the lanes again." Although you can be the most mindful tourist in the world and still be a grockle. You can even live in Devon and have a house and a history and still not belong, because you're missing one word: always.

I passed through the last checkpoint tor and found

myself completely alone with the landscape. After the rush, the moor was noticeably empty and silent.

When we moved to Devon, I did everything I could to fit in. At the local primary school I joined, they treated me with a mixture of curiosity and suspicion. Perhaps that's partly why I threw myself into Dartmoor so hard. Most kids want to fit in and go unnoticed by their peers, but I wanted deeply to belong. I wanted a slice of what they had. So I soaked it all up, the names, the folklore. When we went for family walks I'd proudly recite stories of ghosts and pixies, pointing out each tor by name. But as all playground bullies know, at the root of every harmless taunt is a tiny splinter of pain – if only they can get deep enough to give it a wriggle.

You see, I've always had trouble with belonging. "Where are you from?" seems like such a simple question, but I've never been able to answer it straight. While Devon school friends could give a place, a village – even a country with conviction, I always needed clarification. What exactly do you mean by *from*? Where would you like me to start? I was born in America. Neither of my parents are American and we left when I was two. In fact, I'd lived on three continents before I was three years old. Perhaps you mean ethnically? Genetically? I could never just say, "I'm English." It wasn't that simple.

Technically, by genes, I'm more Dutch than anything. But my Mum was born in Central Africa and moved steadily south as she grew up. My Dad's side is English, with a bit of Irish thrown into the mix. I come from a long line of movers and wanderers. I have family spread across the world. Where am I from? Everywhere in moderation. Nowhere with conviction.

With time people seemed to forget that I hadn't always been there. It felt like being accepted. I wasn't an outsider on the surface any more. I looked pretty local, talked local enough and I even had a local name. My disguise was good, but not quite complete. Invariably when a new acquaintance asked exactly how I fitted into the local Woodhouse clan, I'd blush and admit that I didn't – or at least, not as far as I knew.

By the time I went to university, I'd just say, "I'm from Devon." That's what people meant really: where did you travel from to get here? But I still couldn't quite escape the truth. I went to university in the far north of England and people from the South West were few and far between. There was a certain sense of camaraderie between the handful of us from Devon. It was nice to know people with familiar attitudes and understanding – who just got it. People you could talk to without having to explain or defend the way things were. Particularly in a highly-strung academic environment where everything was seen as the chance for a debate.

One day I was out on a walk by the coast with a Devon friend. Somehow the conversation took a turn into the topic of family origins. I was midway through telling the confusing and exciting story of my family history when he stopped short on the path.

"What is it?" I asked, assuming he'd tripped or dropped something.

"I thought you were from Devon," he exclaimed, sounding cheated. "You know, proper Devon born and bred."

I might have gone to primary school with the postman, but that's still not local enough. I don't have always and there's nothing I can do about it.

As I walked, the mist disappeared and the sun came out with such vigour that I had to stop and apply suncream. I knew the area well so I walked from tor to tor, barely navigating. Climbing Cox Tor, I remembered when this hill had seemed like a mountain, every false summit on the 100 metres of ascent an emotional roller coaster. Although I'd been to Yosemite and stood on top of Table Mountain, I couldn't remember it. They were just stories to me.

I stopped to get some lunch out, a first day celebratory pasty. It was all long-life food after that. I put the pasty down on a rock and tried to pull the bag back on. It was like a slow-motion fight with gravity. I could barely lift it. I could get it off the ground with a yank, but would become stuck around halfway, arms straight. Without quite the strength to heave the monster towards me, I was in a stalemate. But if I caught a shoulder strap, I could swing the bag round in the air, using the momentum to get it over one arm and onto my back. Quickly, I slipped the other arm in and did up the waist belt. I never weighed it. I didn't want to know.

"I really hope I can eat all this!"

My rucksack, and the bulk of its weight, was almost entirely comprised of food. The two litres of water didn't help, but the camping equipment and clothes were negligible by comparison. I'd never really had to calculate that kind of thing before. I just brought enough and ate enough. The longest expedition I'd ever done was the four days spent on my Gold Duke of Edinburgh's Award expedition. It wasn't exactly strenuous walking and we split the food evenly between our group. For this walk I'd multiplied up the calories and filled a supermarket trolley with wraps and dried fruit, biscuits and cereal bars – and emergency jelly babies, of course.

The afternoon wore on and the tor count clocked up. By the time I sat down on White Tor, I'd reached the end of my planned route for the day. Fifteen tors down, 104 to go. It was 3 o'clock. This was where I was meant to be camping.

"Maybe I've set the route card too easy," I thought as I examined my map for options. I couldn't camp here, it was way too early to pitch a tent. The sun was still high and I definitely had room to knock a few more tors off tomorrow's quota. May as well.

I'd brought a little video camera along to record the expedition. This seemed like an appropriate time to pull it out and start filming.

"Hello," I said to the camera. "We're at White Tor… Ha! I'm at White Tor. I just got here and this is where I'm meant to be camping tonight. It's way too early to camp now, so I think I'm going to walk on a bit."

Dartmoor is one of the few places in the UK where it's legal to camp, but it's not quite as simple as throw your tent up anywhere. You can only camp within the allowed boundaries, with a small tent. Plus there are strict rules about not camping too close to a river, road or path – and making sure you arrive late and leave early. I needed to stick to the rules, but a few more tors would do me for today.

At the more appropriate time of evening, just before sunset, I found a flattish spot and pitched my tent. The whole process took me minutes, barely thinking as I put poles into canvas and pegged out the corners. How many nights had I been wild camping now? Hundreds. We'd be out with the Plodders every other weekend a good six months of the year, rain or shine. Or in weather so cold your boot laces froze, for that matter. Setting up camp was an automatic process, like boiling a kettle or brushing your teeth. Even the new tent didn't slow me down.

My tiny three pole tunnel tent was up, fabric rippling gently in the slight breeze. Most of my kit was years old. The tent was the only new bit. It was a super lightweight display model that I was borrowing for the expedition. Lightweight has never really been my thing, but I had cut all the grammes I could to make everything fit in the backpack. It seemed like a sturdy little mountain tent. My only slight concern was that it appeared to have been designed for flat ground. Most of Dartmoor is very lumpy.

Next, I unfurled my roll mat inside the tent and inflated it. Then I laid my down-filled sleeping bag on top, ruffling it up to catch some air and help pre-warm the bag. I put the now empty tent bags inside the inner pocket, along with a drybag full of spare clothes, and did up the inside door zip. Pulling my rucksack under the tent porch, I took out my cooking equipment and then zipped up the outer door too.

Tent set, I found a flat rock and positioned my little gas stove on top of it. The stove was tall and thin. The mug-shaped pan slotted into the top of the burner, the burner screwed into the gas canister and the whole thing balanced on a clever little removable tripod. I poured river water into the pot, lit the gas with a spark and set the water to boil. The stove made a pleasantly familiar roaring noise as I turned up the heat.

In a short while, steam was billowing out of the slot in the lid. My meal tonight – and every night for the duration of the trip – was a dehydrated ration pack, bought in yet another an effort to save weight. It's a meal in a bag, no cooking and no mess. I poured the boiling water into an open pouch, stirred, fished out the oxygen absorber sachet and resealed the pack, setting a timer for 15 minutes. While I waited, I packed away the stove and sat listening to the evening noises. It was quiet but not silent. The nearby sheep chatted about their days, unseen birds chirped and insects buzzed about. A river babbled softly in the distance.

The truth is, I'd never been wild camping alone before. I felt like I was supposed to be worried about it – everyone else seemed to be. A couple of weeks ago, an article about my forthcoming challenge had been placed in the local paper. It was met with lots of concern for my safety. One old lady had gone as far as advising me to take a long knife against intruders in the night. I didn't have a long knife. I had a penknife long enough for slicing apples. But the chances of anyone coming out here tonight were zero. Even with a public tracking map, it wasn't like anyone was actually watching it. People have got far better things to do than troop across Dartmoor to scare solo campers.

Licking my spoon clean, I packed up all my cooking equipment and pulled everything under the tent porch. There was just enough room. Then I unzipped the inner compartment and sat down to take my boots off. I got changed into clean thermals and crawled into my snuggly warm sleeping bag. I stuffed my spare clothes inside a fleece and tied it shut with a hair tie. A Dartmoor Plodder never brings a pillow.

The tent was so small I couldn't quite sit upright and not much longer than I am tall. There wasn't really space to do anything but sleep. So I lay prostrate in my sleeping bag and ticked off today's completed tors from the paper list I'd printed. Then I looked at tomorrow's route by torchlight before settling down for the night.

CHAPTER 4 – FOG

An early morning fog hung over the hills as I packed away my tent. Just like yesterday, I thought, it'll burn away soon. But before the fog lifted, I walked straight up into it. What started as a light haze quickly turned into zero visibility. Standing on the summit stack of Hare Tor, a sea of grey cloud swirled below me. I got my compass out.

"Well this looks a bit serious."

Never had it occurred to me that I'd have any difficulty finding the tors. Not once. Despite all the time I'd spent rescuing people from the fog year round – including August Bank Holiday – it simply hadn't crossed my mind. This was an endurance challenge, not a navigational one. I'd planned lovely long ridgelines, paths and familiar ground at every opportunity. Fat lot of good that was in this weather.

This was foggy. Really foggy. Foggy in a way that is

affectionately known as a 'pea soup-er'. Not that it is particularly green or warm and wholesome. But it is very slow to walk through. I'd stumbled upon the top stack of Hare Tor simply because I knew it had a mast on it. The cloud had closed in as I reached the rocks and soon there was no knowing exactly which direction I'd come from.

This was no time to go wandering around in the mist. I pulled on my red waterproof jacket against the hanging damp and set my compass to the map. All ready to do some serious navigation – wait! In a moment's panic I clutched at the shoulder strap of my rucksack. My fingers found a black shoelace, strung with a set of beads. Phew. So blind was I to the chance of bad visibility that these pacing beads hadn't even made it onto my kit list. Now they were my lifeline.

I scrambled down off the rocks. Inside the cloud everything was coated in a fine layer of rain, like being in a cold sauna. With my big bag, I was precariously top-heavy. I wobbled about on the loose clitter before making it back to grass. Wiping the drizzle off my map, I took a distance, a bearing and a deep breath.

"Right then. One, two, three..."

Pacing is one of the primary tools in a navigator's tool box. It sounds simple in theory: if you know how many of your double paces are in 100 metres, you simply count multiples until you get there. I have 60 double paces to my 100 metres, a conveniently round number. If you can stick to the direction of your bearing and be consistent with your pacing, you can find a paper plate in a field. Trust me, I've had to do it. With every 100 metres travelled, you move a bead along the string to help keep track over long distances.

I'd first learnt the technique on my Mountain Leader Training, but it had really come into its own on Dartmoor. In the Lake District, it's only a matter of metres before you bump into a rock, a tarn or fall off a cliff. On Dartmoor it's possible to pace for miles and miles in a straight line. A lot of the time, especially in weather like this, it was all you had to go on.

Six hundred metres on 352 degrees, 3600 paces: Sharp Tor. Six hundred and fifty metres on 54 degrees, 3900 paces: Chat Tor. The hours went by. The higher I got, the closer and thicker the cloud became. I walked through a bright sea of grey. As soon as I lost sight of the tor behind me, I'd be alone, isolated in a bubble of emptiness, until the next one appeared ghostly out of the fog. In between, I could have been anywhere. Every pace in every direction looked the same: pastel grey meeting tufty brown grass. But the tors kept appearing at the end of each stretch, right where they should be.

Focus. Bearing, pacing, don't lose count. Move the beads, keep walking.

Five tors found out of the day's 18, I sat down and pulled out a Penguin bar.

"What do you call 500 penguins in Trafalgar Square?" I smiled. It was my favourite. "Lost… What do you call one Emily on Dartmoor? Not lost yet."

A few hours later, I was less sure of the fact. The grey wash across my canvas of vision all but covered the page, leaving only a thin brown line by my feet. If I reached out,

I'd start to lose my hand in the mist. This was some of the worst I'd ever seen it on Dartmoor – or rather, not seen it.

"What the hell am I supposed to pace off?"

There was almost nothing left to line a bearing up on. A tuft of grass two metres away, then the next and the next...

For my final navigation assessment, the last hurdle to get into Dartmoor Rescue, the weather had been terrible. I'm fairly sure they arrange it that way with Dartmoor. As night fell, the rain had been horizontal and the visibility was down to eight metres. No exaggeration: I know because I paced it. At least today I had daylight. At least it wasn't raining like it meant it. I'd passed my navigation assessment and I could pass this.

That's what I told myself as I hauled a trapped foot back out of yet another ditch, hidden under dead heather, long grass and gorse. The sludgy brown dregs of summer under a grey haze. Easy to break an ankle in. I wondered how long it would take for someone to notice if I got into trouble out here. Even with the tracker location marked, it would take hours for anyone to reach me.

I had a bit of a navigational wobble by Great Links Tor and Little Links Tor, mistaking one for the other. The video camera was fast becoming a companion on this journey. By talking through my logic to it, as if it was another person, it became clear which was the right course of action. Or more specifically how ridiculous it sounded to base my identification of a tor solely on a small hollow. So what if it looked like the one we'd sat in for mulled wine last Christmas? It turned out my pacing was coming up a good hundred metres short over rough ground, probably because of the weight of my rucksack. But my bearings were good and if I just took the extra distance into account I was back on target.

"Normal service has resumed," I announced to the camera with a grin. I'd made it across the hillside to Kitty Tor.

Fifteen minutes later, when I arrived at the actual tor, I beat myself up for my stupidity.

"Don't get complacent, Emily."

The next bit was going to be difficult. The last time I'd been out here, I'd done the leg in reverse, navigating from Hunt Tor to Kitty Tor. It was a freezing January night, just weeks before my final navigation assessment with Dartmoor Rescue. Steve, a fellow Team member, who'd passed the winter before, was out keeping me company and helping me practise. Confidently pacing out along the disused railway track to our start point, I'd put my foot down on a patch of ice in the dark. I was on the floor before I knew what had happened, all illusions of competence shattered and pacing count forgotten.

The trouble was, around here the map wanted to trick you. There were lots of really convenient looking paths marked exactly the same way as the dismantled railway line. Except they weren't. While they might look resplendent in all their double-dashed glory from the sky, on the ground they were barely traceable. They 'existed' in various degrees from paved highway to slight impression in the grass. In between these 'paths' were wide plains of undulating bog, wrapped in ankle-binding dead grass, criss-crossed with ditches and ancient tin workings. It was a wasteland. Bleugh.

I looked at the tantalising double-dashed track marked on the map between Kitty and Hunt Tor. I was fairly certain it wasn't there. But the dream of not wading through dead grass and bog was too strong.

"I'll just take a bearing along it," I told myself. "Then if it's there I win and if it isn't I'm still going in the right direction."

That was a great plan, right up until I thought I'd found the path, stopped pacing and then discovered I hadn't found it. Ah great. So began a series of guestimations as to how far I'd walked before I needed to take a sharp left across the plain to Hunt Tor. All the while, the fog was as thick as ever.

This is not how to navigate. The key component to not getting lost is to make a plan and stick to it. Sounds almost too simple. Be a machine, follow the instructions – and yet the human brain does everything it can to conspire against you. Plan? What plan? Never mind that. I'm sure we've been here before. That way looks familiar. Let's go along this thing that looks like a path. Oh look it's not a path... oops. Never mind. How about this one? I'm sure it goes in the right direction...

Surely the intuition of a hardened Mountain Jedi, with years of varied experience and finely honed skills, knows better? Absolutely not. Our brains have infinite capacity to convince ourselves of things. That's what they're designed to do, after all: create a theory and find things to back that theory up, not refute it. You get used to ignoring that bit of your head while you're navigating, but you can never really turn it off.

Not quite at the level of wandering aimlessly around in the fog, I patched together a plan until I found myself at the end of my pacing in a shallow bowl in the otherwise featureless moorland. Outside of the bowl was fog. I could have been in a tiny dip on a plain or at the bottom of a slope. It was impossible to tell.

"Ah."

I'd already gone an extra 100 metres over my measured pacing – not that it means anything much when you're working off a guestimate. Local knowledge can only get you so far in the fog, but this was definitely not Hunt Tor. Had I overshot or not gone far enough?

"Oh flip."

I had no idea where I was and no way of telling. Standing in the empty landscape, it hit home just how isolated I was. There was no one nearby for miles. No help or back up for hours and hours. I had to sort this out on my own. This was between me and Dartmoor. Dartmoor had made its move. Now it was my turn.

But I didn't know what to do. I simply didn't have enough information to go off. I'd been too complacent. This would be the end of my reputation as a navigator. I imagined all my friends watching the tracker in real time, pointing and laughing.

"Haha look, she's over there! And she's trying to get to Hunt Tor!" What a joke.

The tracker was public. The record of my blunder would be there forever. They had all the answers. They knew exactly where I was but they wouldn't tell me. They couldn't tell me. No one could help me right now. Not that I really believed anyone was actually following my tracker at all.

I had no idea what to do. So I stood in the fog and the wind, as if waiting for a sign. This would be the moment for the cloud to miraculously lift and reveal my tor, ideally in a clear shaft of sunlight. But it didn't. Dartmoor didn't like me. I'd got myself into this mess and I was the only one who could get me out of it. Somehow.

But I didn't need any of them, did I? That was why I was here in the first place. I had the necessary skills to get myself out of this situation without running for help or cheating. Not that I had any way of cheating. All I had was a map and compass. It was solve the problem or give up. It would be easy to panic, but I wasn't going to.

I looked back down at the map. This is your thing. You've got this.

Eventually I decided that – if anything – I was probably too far east and maybe too far south. I could at least get out of this bowl and see if it was the start of a hill or not. I took a sight bearing uphill and walked 100 metres. Still no tor. More giggles from the tracker watchers. I squinted into the distance. But then, there was something – an outline in the mist... maybe? I walked another 100 metres, careful to stay on the same bearing. At about 50 metres, a dark shape loomed out of the mist. I reached it before I'd counted to 60. It was Hunt Tor.

I leant forward and touched the wet granite.

"Thank you Dartmoor."

CHAPTER 5 – STORM

The sheep seemed to know where it was going. I followed it. We scrambled through the undergrowth over huge granite blocks, down towards the river.

An hour and a half after finding Hunt Tor and only two more tors in the bag, I'd sat down behind the trig point on Sourton Tor. Back to the wind, I leant against my rucksack to take the pressure off my shoulders.

"I am so fed up of counting!" I shouted. I'd counted every step I'd taken in the past six hours and it was starting to drive me insane.

Dartmoor didn't reply. The wind kept up. The fog stayed low. Wearily, I hauled my rucksack onto my back and plodded on. Four more tors to go.

That was how I'd found myself scrambling over the mess of boulders below Black Tor. I had cut a corner. It served me right. I was on the way to my last tor and I just wanted the day to be over. Instead of avoiding the obvious disaster, clearly marked on the map, I was stumbling down a hillside through clitter on steroids. This was ankle breaking territory. Some rocks were so big and my bag so top-heavy that I had to sit down and lower myself into the gap below. Bracken and other dense plants grew out of the holes, hiding how deep they were. Everywhere looked awful, so if it was good enough for sheep, it was probably good enough for me.

Once, on Ten Tors training, we'd met an Army guy below Oke Tor. He'd taken the trouble of walking over to instruct us not to navigate off sheep. Don't line your bearings up on them. They move. Even at the age of 14, we were all very bemused. Now here I was following a sheep. But then I'd never thought much of his advice. He'd also insisted that we must carry at least six pairs of socks for the weekend and stop to change every time they got wet. We'd all agreed that if we did that, we'd never get anywhere. Walking on Dartmoor was synonymous with wet feet. A decade later, my opinion hadn't changed. I was spending 10 days on Dartmoor with just three pairs of socks.

Finally, I reached Lints Tor, my finishing spot for the night. My route card had one more tor for the day, but I thought I'd take a gamble. No point in pushing on now in the fog when tomorrow morning could be clear. Weather like this rarely stuck around for days on end. I would be smart and save the last tor for the morning. Plus I needed somewhere out of the wind to camp tonight. The remnants of a hurricane was coming through, as forecast, with winds up to 50 miles per hour. The Met Office had issued weather warnings liberally across the start of the week.

I arrived at Lints Tor as it was getting dark. The day had left me exhausted. Although I'd finally stopped pacing, the numbers still rolled around in my head like a catchy song you can't get rid of. The storm was meant to hit soon and I frantically searched for a sheltered place to pitch.

The rocks of the tor itself were not as high or sheer as on many. There was no tall stack of granite to hide behind. What did stick out above the ground was embedded into the grass hillside in a series of small ledges. With the wind coming from the south west, I desperately tried to find a place with some protection from the elements – any protection.

Three times I tried to pitch the tent. The first time, the tent was too large to fit in the spot I'd picked. The second, it was at too much of an angle and there was a huge clump of reeds growing on the only flat bit nearby. I went to slash at the reeds with a penknife before realising that was a stupid idea in more ways than one. I thought about going on to Dinger Tor. Was the shelter any better? I racked my brains for the exact orientation of the tor. It had been years since I'd been there. But I couldn't remember and I didn't want to risk walking all the way up there, only for it to be worse. At least Lints Tor was an isolated lump near the valley bottom. The wind would be much worse higher up.

Finally, I went right down off the tor and squeezed my tent in at an angle under the bottom ledge, barely higher than the tent. All around me were reeds and lumpy tussock grass. The wind was growing. It would have to do.

I crawled into the tent, realising at just how interesting an angle I'd pitched it. My head was uphill, but the whole tent was twisted over sideways, as if being slowly tipped off a slope. As soon as I placed my inflated roll mat on the ground, it slid across the smooth floor and down to the bottom corner of the tent. Guess that's where I'd end up in the morning.

I pulled everything into the tent, did up the porch zip and just sat there. I was so glad the day was over. Now I could relax. Except I hadn't cooked dinner yet. That was a bad idea, getting into the tent before cooking dinner. Hugging my knees, I listened to the slap of rain against the fabric and watched as the frame shook in the wind. Getting my stove to stay lit, never mind stay upright, was going to be a challenge. I simply couldn't face it.

Settling for a cold dinner of wraps and snacks, I took off my damp socks and hung them on the line just above me. They danced around as the tent shook from side to side. The tent may have been ultralight, but it was proving to be sturdy. There was no sign of poles breaking or fabric coming undone. I'd slept in some bad places before. Between the two of us, we could make it through the night. It was fine, but I really wanted to get some good sleep. Hopefully I was exhausted enough to sleep through the bad conditions. I really needed it.

The strange angle of the slope meant that the two layers of the tent, the inner fabric and the outer fabric, were closer than normal. A gust of wind could push them together, allowing water to get through where they touched. This needed to be fixed. So early in the expedition, I had to protect my dry belongings as much as possible. For all I knew it could be raining solidly for the next week – although I really hoped not.

The storm was coming in. Frantically but methodically, I tried to fix the tent. How can I separate the inner and the outer? I reached out between the two layers and undid some of the elasticated clips, trying to create more of a gap on the windward side. The inner sagged, but the loose fabric just flapped even more. What about a physical barrier? I manoeuvred my inflated roll mat into the gap. But there was nothing to stop it from sliding down the tent wall. All this achieved was getting my mat wet. I pulled it back in and dried it off with my fleece.

Finally, I settled on keeping some clips undone and tying up the excess fabric with a spare hair tie. The tent still shook, but it stopped the flapping. The water didn't seem to be getting through as much. That would have to do. Again, I sat still in the tent, one long plait of hair slowly unwinding of its own accord. My brain was spiralling. What if the weather was going to be like this for the entire expedition? What if I had to navigate like today for the next 10 days? I'd only just kept up with the route card today and it had almost broken me mentally. I finished my dinner and got into my sleeping bag, watching the socks jerk ever more erratically on the line above my face. The tent shook dramatically.

I lay still.

56… 57… 58… Oh shut up.

Most of all, I just wanted to know that the weather was

going to be better tomorrow. Send the rain-pocalypse by all means, but I needed to see more than 100 metres ahead. Pacing was methodical but slow and mentally draining. You never got a chance to switch off. If only I could check the weather, but there was no phone signal here. Alone in a tiny tent in a dark valley, battered by the storm, I was completely cut off from the world. No one to get my back. No one to cheer me up or tell me that tomorrow would be a better day.

I'd got what I wanted. I was very, very alone.

The next morning, bleary-eyed from lack of sleep, I unzipped my tent door. Crouching in the porch, I peered around the corner to check the weather. Fog. An imposing wall of grey hung down thick in front of the hillside. Exactly like yesterday.

"Oh get lost!" I shouted angrily and got back into the tent.

CHAPTER 6 – COW

I sat on top of Steeperton Tor in the mid-afternoon sun. Below me stretched a glorious view out over Dartmoor to the horizon. Hiding from the wind behind the little military hut, I watched a rainbow appear across the North Moor. This is what I'd signed up for.

"I love Dartmoor."

After a grim and murky start, I'd been standing on the highest point of Dartmoor before 9 am. The view from Yes Tor was pure cloud.

"Look at this stunning view!" I'd quipped to the camera, "You can almost imagine you're in the Lake District." Or on any British mountain, for that matter.

Then something amazing happened. As I descended off Yes Tor, I dropped out of the bottom of the cloud that I'd been stuck in for over a day. I could see again. Yes it was wet and windy, but I could see. Tucking my compass back into a pocket, I tied up my pacing beads and walked straight for my next tor. West Mill Tor: a kilometre away and in plain sight.

From there, the day had only got better and by mid-afternoon I was walking under a deep blue sky. I figured that was probably it for the bad weather. The storm had passed and we'd be back to the stable, mild weather we'd had for weeks beforehand. I'd proved my worth to Dartmoor and now we could get back to a standard September.

The sunshine made everything better. There was not much left on today's schedule. I casually passed through the end of my 14 tor quota. As I took a little break at Watern Tor, my thirteenth for the day, I felt like everything was back under control. It was only mid-afternoon and I was comfortably within time. I could dry the tent in this wind, dry my socks and boots – and cook dinner all before it got dark. Luxurious.

Between Watern Tor and Hound Tor the land makes a swooping, broad basin. The tufty grass hillside curves round like a bowl and slopes down to a deep bog at the bottom that seeps out around the Walla Brook. The path between the two tors curves gently round the inside of the basin, avoiding the bog without too much extra ascent.

With my mind already preoccupied, deciding which dehydrated delicacy I would be having for dinner, I strolled down the path from Watern Tor. There was a herd of twenty or so brown cows in the bowl below me. They were spread out along the hillside and round the corner, generally above and to the left of the path, happily munching their afternoon tea. They were thinly scattered between the rocks and tussock grass, perhaps looking for delicacies of their own.

A couple of cows, at the very end of this line, had strayed quite close to the path down from Watern Tor.

"Excuse me," I said cautiously as I approached, hoping they would move.

You have to be careful with cows. It's something everyone says, particularly when they have calves. There are horror stories, but it's not something I'd actually seen evidence of. No one I knew had ever had any trouble with cows. There are many herds roaming unattended on Dartmoor, although they don't outnumber the sheep.

I edged forwards a little. These cows were not budging. They also couldn't care a less about my existence. Grass was far more exciting. I looked out across the wide spread of the herd. There were no calves that I could see. So I walked slowly forwards, at a fair distance, talking placidly to the cows all the time. They completely ignored me.

I passed them and continued merrily along the path. The sun was shining, I was mostly out of the wind and, in the immortal words of The Lego Movie, everything was awesome. Since no one was around for miles, I started quietly singing to myself. Today was a much better day. I glanced over my shoulder, just in time to see 500 tonnes of cow hurtling down the hillside towards me. What? Without time to think, I screamed and sprinted straight downhill into the bog. This also happened to be the trajectory line of the cow.

I reached the bog. There were long upright stalks of

some dead plant sticking out, but I went crashing through, stumbling forwards into the reeds, trying not to trip. My overloaded rucksack toppled me off balance, trying to knock me to the ground. If I hit the floor the bag would be little defence against the cow. The bog was deep but I hurtled forwards, trying to keep my feet off the ground, trying not to lose them into sinkholes of light green moss. I managed a few more leaps before I had to stop or tumble. Stumbling to a halt, I dared a glance behind, bracing myself to be pinned to the ground and trampled to death.

The cow reached the edge of the bog and slowed, stopped. I stared at it and it stared back. The cow seemed satisfied that the threat had been dealt with. Throwing its head up in disgust, it waddled back over to the herd.

Heart pounding and eyes wide, I stood in the middle of the bog, slowly sinking under the weight of my rucksack. What just happened? Why had it charged me? I didn't do anything! What if I hadn't turned around? Why did I turn around in the first place? I didn't hear it coming. What if it had hit me? I tried to slow my breathing down. No one would ever have known. I can't let my guard down. Ever. Dartmoor is trying to kill me.

Hiding in the reeds, I watched the cow rejoin its herd. It wasn't a cow. It was a bull. Since when had there been bulls out on Dartmoor? And there were the baby cows too, way out at the other end of the herd, playing hide and seek in the rocks. Trying to catch me out.

I skulked across the bog and out up the other side of the hill to Hound Tor.

CHAPTER 7 – SAVANNAH

The night did not go well. Although my tent dried quickly, the wind came in stronger and stronger as night fell. There was no protection from the tor. When I'd almost fallen asleep, a gust of wind would flick a drop of water from outside, through the inner and onto my face. Every time. Eventually the wind was so strong that I ended up dragging my tent round to the other side of the tor in the middle of the night. This was fine, if a little desperate, until I realised I had left some things in the porch. Luckily, I found my spoon and lighter in the morning dew.

It did at least stop raining, although it was still very wet underfoot. My feet had assumed a strange new wrinkly existence, bright white and puffy, soles fixed into furrows like windblown sand. Some early morning misdirection in the bog only made matters worse. It seemed impossible to keep my feet dry.

At Rival Tor, there was a cow and calf right on the summit. I got close enough that no one could claim I hadn't been there, but I didn't physically touch the rock. I chose life. Before long, it was raining again. I spent a glamorous 15 minutes outside the public toilets at Fernworthy Reservoir, eating crushed naan bread as the rain dripped from the awning. The toilets were locked and I was devastated. I'd run out of water and there were no streams until the end of the day. Then I was treated to more fog on the way to camp, just to top it off.

Now, on day five with 60 tors completed, I was walking through an area I'd never been to in my life. Yesterday's low cloud had been replaced by blue skies and 60 mph winds, coming directly from the west. It was as if Dartmoor knew I'd just turned a corner. I was walking straight into it.

Wading through head high bracken, I was running late. I was supposed to be meeting Savannah from Dartmoor National Park at Leigh Tor this morning. That was why the most direct route had seemed like a good idea. Now I was trapped. How was I supposed to know they had such a bracken problem out here? Thrashing about, I tried to pull my legs out of the tangle of brambles growing underneath, without ripping my trousers. This was unheard of on my side of Dartmoor.

"I concede!" I exclaimed, flailing at the long stems, trying to find my way back to safety.

I wanted to sit down and hide, but there was nowhere to rest here. The floor was completely covered in brambles and I was standing knee deep in it. Plus I only had a few minutes left to get up the hill and meet Savannah. Mike had mentioned some PR photos at the start, helping to promote responsible camping on Dartmoor. Not that I was feeling particularly photogenic right now. Although if I showed up with my clothes torn and hair full of bracken, it would at least be an accurate representation of how I felt.

Finally, I made it back onto the main path, vowing I would never leave the path again in this part of Dartmoor. I arrived on Leigh Tor, breathless, looking like I'd had a battle with a hedge. The bunch of kids on a rock climbing excursion didn't seem particularly impressed. I looked about. No Savannah, just a hoard of kids in numbered helmets and matching harnesses. Was this even the right place? I double checked the map and, yes, this was it. I sat down and waited. Dropping my rucksack, I started to pull bits of Dartmoor out of my hair. If I didn't have a tick by now, I'd be amazed.

It was the first time I'd really stopped in days, except to eat or sleep. Gazing out to the east, I thought about that moody row of hills I'd seen in the distance yesterday. It was, I was sure, going to be the most contentious decision in my classification of 'all'.

You see, claiming to do 'all' the tors was already pretty controversial. Unlike the Munros of Scotland or the Wainwrights in the Lake District, there is no hard and fast definition of a tor. No one can agree on how many there are because no one can agree on what 'counts'. There is no measurement involved: no height or size or prominence requirements. A granite outcrop could be huge or tiny.

Where do you draw the line? Some enthusiastic locals have clocked up a list of over 700 rocks and outcrops. This appears to be a quest to catalogue every rock and stone on Dartmoor, regardless of size. Of course, very few of these appear on maps distinctly and fewer still with names. But there are many locally used place names that have never made it onto a Dartmoor map. Or have made it onto some but not others. Rather than get dragged into the ever narrowing scale of obscurity, I drew a line. It had to be on the Ordnance Survey Dartmoor map and it had to be named as a tor. No rocks or beacons or hills: tors.

But Dartmoor National Park is far bigger than the area most people would call Dartmoor. It includes a whole host of towns and villages and isolated tors, surrounded by fields but weirdly with open access. There was no way I could include all those and legally camp along the way too. Plus spending hours walking along roads wasn't really in the spirit of what I was doing. So I'd settled on all the tors in the big connected bit in the middle, which is what most people would call Dartmoor anyway.

To my surprise, the ridgeline that included Hound Tor, Pil Tor and Haytor Rocks wasn't actually attached to the main part of Dartmoor. Despite being the place where most tourists stop to tick Dartmoor off their bucket list, you couldn't get from there to the rest of the moor without crossing through private land. Or walking along the road through Widecombe, I suppose. I knew people would moan, but it felt somehow right for those tors not to be a part of the challenge.

Looking out at that line of hills, they'd certainly looked like tors, dark and foreboding under the cloud – grumpy even at being left out of my walk. After so many days of visiting tors, my sensors had been fine tuned. So it wasn't that. Why not include them then? Well, for a start, they certainly weren't wild enough.

It used to drive me mad at university. So often, when I mentioned Dartmoor, I'd get the same shallow response.

"Oh yeah, I've been there," they'd say. "We parked at Haytor and had an icecream, then went home."

A thin strip of moorland surrounded by towns, roads and fields simply wasn't isolated enough to be proper Dartmoor. It had been tamed. But then here, on the very edge of my chosen boundary, it didn't feel particularly isolated or wild either. Maybe I should have included it. But adding even one exception would be a slippery slope away from a clear definition.

I watched another small face pop up over the top of the Leigh Tor rock and then I hit on it: Ten Tors. That's what this is really about. Taking Ten Tors to its most extreme limits. Would Ten Tors routes ever include that strip east of Widecombe? No. Would the Army ever train there? I highly doubted it.

My musings were interrupted by a voice from behind.

"Sorry I'm late!" said the puffing voice behind a large camera bag and tripod.

"Savannah? Hey, nice to meet you."

It turned out that, in a series of Dartmoor Whispers, I was actually having a video interview about the walk so far. We did the best we could with the high wind, hiding behind the tor. I put on a smile and tried not to look quite as exhausted as I felt. It had been a long time since I'd had to verbalise my thoughts or answer questions. I'd barely seen another person in days.

Footage successfully recorded, I walked with Savannah back to the car park, then carried on my way.

CHAPTER 8 – INDECISION

The wind was severe. Already bent at 45 degrees as I reached the shelter of Mel Tor, it didn't take much to topple me onto the floor. Relieved, I jettisoned my rucksack and crawled over to the edge of the tor, to peer down into the Dart Valley.

The ground dropped away steeply to the left. Separating me from the river was head high bracken, followed by a defensive strip of gorse bushes that finally merged into trees. After that, who knew. Eyes streaming, I tried to make out a route down. There was no path that I could see. Bald patches of grass up top, descending quickly into a spiky, tick infested jungle. Yuck.

Flat on my stomach, squinting into the wind, it looked hopeless. It had been one of the vaguer bits of my route plan, but I hadn't expected this. I certainly couldn't see a tor – although the map told me that somewhere down there was a forsaken lump of granite known as Luckey Tor. I was not feeling particularly lucky. I was still in a section of the moor that I knew barely anything about. This next section was a bit of a loose end that I'd optimistically tied up and assumed would be doable. This is Dartmoor, after all, there's not a lot it can reasonably throw in your way. After hours spent bashing through bracken, I knew differently.

Turning my face back out of the wind, I huddled behind a rock and pulled out a cereal bar. Munching on my indecision, I propped my throbbing feet up off the ground. Going even slightly off piste in my rush to meet Savannah had been terrible. Unworkable, as we'd say over the radio. Relocate to a better position and try again. But all the paths leading to Luckey Tor came up from the River Dart. I'd have to fight my way down from above or walk some seven kilometres round and probably the same back again. That just wasn't an option.

Cereal bar finished, I rolled back over for another look. I didn't fancy having another bracken-bramble fight again (ever). If Leigh Tor was standard, then this looked like the next level of pain. All that plus haggard old gorse bushes, trees with branches drooping to the floor and no path to speak of. I peeked over the lip of the rock to triple check. Nothing. My heart sank.

I ducked back down out of the wind again and crawled back to the safety of the tor and my bag. At what point does a tor count as inaccessible? The rules already only included tors in the main Open Access Land, which I was abbreviating to "accessible". Only accessible tors on the map.

Sounds very reasonable. Plus, I didn't actually physically touch the rock on Rival Tor two days ago. So technically I didn't have to actually touch Luckey Tor either, just get close enough. There was definitely no path from here to there – or any way through without a chainsaw and an industrial lawnmower, both of which I'd sadly forgotten to pack. If only they had a few more sheep around here.

I remembered Bob describing part of this area as a "bit of a bracken bash". Bob is a six foot something retired policeman in Dartmoor Rescue. His bash looked more like a swim to me. But then we were always mock-bickering about something. Bob is a tor bagger, reaching what I feel is near the upper echelons of pedantic. It's a common trait amongst people who deeply love the moors.

If in doubt of a person's Dartmoor Nerd rating, a good test is to ask them, "What's the highest tor on Dartmoor?" Most people would simply answer Yes Tor. A Grade One Dartmoor Nerd might argue for High Willhays but concede if you insisted it had to have Tor in the name. Bob and other Grade Two Dartmoor Nerds insist it's High Willhays and, if it really must include Tor, then it's Hampster Tor – a part of High Willhays that is on nobody's map. Most locals have never heard of it.

I imagined trying to explain to Bob why I couldn't get to Luckey Tor. He'd chuckle and look down at me over his glasses, "Oh, you could have done it."

"But I couldn't find a way through all the bushes and trees and bracken. It was inaccessible."

"Ah, you definitely could have done it," he'd grin in mock

sincerity. "You'll have to go back."

Sitting with my back against Mel Tor, I imagined going home after all this and explaining to everyone why I'd skipped Luckey Tor.

"There were impenetrable gorse bushes.

"The bracken was taller than me!

"I was really tired and it was ridiculously windy and my feet hurt..."

They all sounded like hollow excuses, even to my ears.

"I was nearly there. I got close enough to see it."

I thought of all the times I'd had to tell off cocky 55 teams who hadn't actually gone to their checkpoints. Being able to see the top of Sittaford Tor is not the same as going to it. Especially when there's a cold, wet leader waiting for you on top.

The voices in my head kept going. This time, though, they were other people's.

"Seriously, Emm, I thought you were more hardcore."

"Oh, I see, that's a bit disappointing..."

"So you didn't do all the tors to start with and then you couldn't even manage those. What a grockle."

I considered the responses glumly.

People don't remember the suffering you went through to reach a goal. They remember the result. Did you win or did you fail? Did you make the cut, or didn't you? No retreat. No surrender. I had to go down.

Decision made, I stalled one more time by flipping open the camera. To make it official, I told myself. Pale faced and puffy-eyed, I stared down the lens.

"I've just got to keep going, right?" I sighed. "Can't say I did All the Tors Except One because it was a bit difficult to get to."

It was time. I pulled on my rucksack from seated and half rolled, half dragged myself onto my feet. Assuming the 45 degree wind offensive position, I stepped out from behind the tor.

CHAPTER 9 – LUCKEY

It was bad. For want of a better idea, I'd chosen to stay close to a wall that ran out west along the top of the valley. It could help get me started before I cut straight downhill to Luckey Tor. I couldn't use it forever, but it was a good start. Something to cling to, at least, while navigating the jungle. Plus if anyone had made a path through this mess, I figured they'd probably have put it along the wall. That's what they'd done on Leigh Tor.

After making it through the first thicket of thorns, I found the wall and started to thrash my way along it through the undergrowth. There was no path. I found myself in a tangle of spindly trees and bushes, some looking like they'd escaped out of someone's garden. If I'd had a fight with a hedge before, now I was taking on the whole wood.

I couldn't see the floor for the greenery. At one point I was doing the limbo under a tree branch, wearing a 60 litre rucksack. Of course, this didn't end well. My feet slipped out from under me and I found myself lying on my back like a turtle. This was ridiculous.

Finally, still in sight of the wall, I bulldozed my way out into a clearing. Beside me was a friendly brown wooden door, someone's back gate. Better still, the clearing was a thin strip – a path from the door down into the woods. It wasn't quite in the right direction, but at this point I would take any help I could get. I followed it down towards the Dart.

Eventually, much lower down the slope, the bracken shrunk back to stompable heights. As it shrank, big trees with silvery white bark grew up in their place and higher up into a canopy. Thin tree limbs reached out in all directions, hanging thick with moss. It felt like no one had disturbed them in years. Tangly plants snagged around my boots, catching on my gaiter straps, tripping me up.

I stumbled on until, finally, I saw it. A pathetic lump of moss-covered granite, hidden under trees and grass at the edge of a cliff.

"Is that it!" I exclaimed, underwhelmed.

I got a bit closer to check it was definitely a tor and not just a rock. Nope, this was it. Riled, I took a picture as evidence and turned straight back around.

It's a good job I didn't go further or I would have found out exactly why people like to visit Luckey Tor, by means of a forty foot drop into the Dart Valley. Apparently the rock face is quite impressive from the river looking up. I had no idea it was there.

"Right. Now how do I get out of here?"

A 20 minute jungle expedition later, I emerged into the light, victorious.

"Ha, take that Luckey Tor."

I figured it would be a good time to have lunch. Get to the next tor and treat yourself. Nothing says celebration quite like a peanut butter wrap.

For the uninitiated, the humble peanut butter wrap is a superfood of expedition lunches – or dinners, or breakfasts! It's got a very efficient space to energy ratio and is good to eat in hot or cold conditions. The wraps do go mouldy after a while though. To preserve my stockpile as best as I could, I was keeping the two magic ingredients separate for as long as possible.

A friend had told me about a trick she'd used for peanut butter on one of her kayaking expeditions. She'd pre-portioned it out into cling film in advance, to save having to bring a glass jar and knife for spreading. New to the whole idea of ultralight backpacking, I thought this sounded like a great idea. The night before the walk I had meticulously portioned out my peanut butter and wrapped it into cling film pods. Then, not wanting to undo my savings by carrying a hard plastic tub, I'd placed them in a ziplock bag in the top pocket of my rucksack. This had worked a treat until the first time I put my bag down against anything solid. Five days in, they were well and truly smushed.

Nevertheless, I sat down on Sharp Tor and extracted half-exploded blobs of peanut butter from the bag. The tor was surrounded by wide grass paths, cutting neatly through the bracken. I sat on the leeward slope, my chosen rock in full sun and mostly out of the wind. There were lots of people around, fooled by the sunshine on the forecast, and I vaguely wondered what they thought of me. But only vaguely. I smeared some peanut butter onto a wrap and licked the cling film clean. From my vantage point, I watched people in jeans and trainers, stumbling from car to tor, into the wind, and back again. Little did they know. Chewing thoughtfully on a wrap, I looked out into the west – the weather was coming.

CHAPTER 10 – STEVE

Someone was walking down the path ahead of me. It was raining again, the cloud settling down for the evening, but not quite foggy yet. The extreme wind had died down as the weather came in, so it felt like a completely different day. In the early evening gloom, I could see the shape of a person wrapped in full waterproofs, a bright blue raincover pulled down over their rucksack. It looked almost familiar. Don't kid yourself, Emily. No one's going to be out here for you in this weather.

I cut off the path to collect one more tor. There was something a bit odd about the way the person was moving. They'd walk a few paces away from me. Stop. Look down for a minute, then carry on. Almost as if they were looking at a GPS trace. Almost as if they were trying to find someone.

I crashed through the heather down from Laughter Tor to get straight back to the path. Reaching it, I sped up, trying to catch this person. I was sure I recognised them, even – especially – in waterproofs and a backpack. The closer I got, the more I thought that there was a luminous yellow raincover peeking out from underneath the blue one.

"I'm over here!" I shouted, but the wind took it away east.

He carried on westwards and so did I. But he wasn't stopping enough. I wouldn't catch up. I heard Stu's voice in my back of my head, that infamous phrase for when we were running behind schedule, "You might need to trot a little..."

I grabbed hold of my shoulder straps, leant forwards and started a strange little shuffle run into the wind. My feet barely left the ground but the pressure change was enough to feel bubbles squeezing out of wet socks between wet toes. It was working though, I was gaining on him. Hood up, he didn't see me coming. I stopped a few paces behind him. I was certain.

"Steve!"

He turned around, "Hello!"

"You found me," I grinned. Search and Rescue at its finest.

"I kept looking at the tracker, like: I know she's got to be around here somewhere. Can I walk with you a bit?"

We walked across to Bellever Tor, my last tor for the day. Just in time really: it was already gloomy with dusk. I pulled out my camera at the top.

"Woah, wait!" said Steve, jumping up. "Let me get out of the way. You're supposed to be solo and unsupported, right? No one should know I've been here."

I shrugged and took a photo of the tor.

"Where are you camping tonight?"

"Over by one of those walls down there. Hopefully out of the wind."

He looked at his watch. "Okay, well I'll see you set up camp alright and then I'll head off. Don't want to be late for training."

Of course, it was Wednesday.

"What's training tonight?"

"NavEx out at Lane End."

"Uh huh. Hey wait – that's a bit of a drive!"

"I'll make it."

We walked in the direction of my chosen camping spot.

"Good night for it," I said. Navigation exercises are always more fun in bad weather.

"Yeah it's clagging in a bit, could be good."

I paused. "Is anyone… are people sort of following me? On my tracker?"

"Oh yeah," exclaimed Steve, "definitely. People are really rooting for you. We were all talking about it down the pub the other night. People think you're nuts, of course, and are seriously impressed that you're doing it in this weather."

"Huh," I said, surprised but not really believing him.

"And there are loads of people commenting on the stuff that they're sharing on the Team's Facebook page. Andy's putting out updates and pictures. People love it. They're calling you Dartmoor's Daughter."

"No they're not, that's someone else."

He shrugged, "Well they are."

"Well they shouldn't be. It's the name of the guiding

company of this lady I bumped into the other day. She took a picture and said she'd share it."

I'd met her with a group of American tourists over by Scorhill Tor on day four. We'd realised we kind of knew each other and, after a brief moment's fangirl-ing over Dartmoor, gone our separate ways.

We reached my chosen wall. I threw my bag off and started emptying it out onto the grass to reach the tent.

"Can I help with anything?" asked Steve.

I smiled at him, "You literally cannot help. That would be cheating."

Within a few minutes, I'd pitched the tent and stood, hands on hips, inspecting it like an artist examines their creation. One tweak here or one tweak there might stop it from sagging in the night.

"I brought you some stuff."

I turned to see that Steve had emptied out his own bag too. Beside a helmet and goggles was a carrier bag full of sweets and chocolate.

"Here," he said. "For you. Take whatever you like."

Oh heck, now this really was cheating. I smiled and looked inside the bag. There was a colourful assortment of biscuits and bars, sweets and chocolate. I took out a bag of jelly babies and a big sharing bar of chocolate, just to be polite.

"Are you sure?"

"Definitely, take it."

"Thanks," I said again. "That's really kind. Hey, maybe we can swap? I've got some stuff in here I'm never going to eat."

I could have dumped it in the bins at Postbridge tomorrow morning, but it seemed a shame to waste the food. There was nothing wrong with it except it was unnecessarily heavy.

"Okay," agreed Steve.

I pulled out a carrier bag full of my entire porridge rations for the trip. At halfway, I still hadn't managed to eat even one of them. Then I added a couple of dehydrated ration packs, from nights I'd missed dinner, and a bag of wraps.

"Are you sure you're not going to need this?"

"I'm never going to eat it. I massively over packed on food."

This is not strictly true. I'd very carefully calorie counted before the trip. But the weather was against me cooking and I simply couldn't eat it all fast enough.

It was getting late and Steve needed to get to training. He packed up his stuff, squeezing in my spare food, and disappeared off into the night. I was left sitting alone in the dark and the rain, grinning from ear to ear.

CHAPTER 11 - FLOOD

The following morning I had only one question on my mind: Waterfall or Sandy Hole Pass? It was going to be a wet day. The cloud that had settled overnight showed no signs of leaving. I packed up my tent in the morning dew, indistinguishable from the hanging blanket of damp over Dartmoor.

Between Sittaford Tor and Lower White Tor, there is a river called the East Dart, one of the two tributaries of the River Dart and a fairly major river in its own right. There are no bridges across the East Dart, except way down off the moor at Postbridge. But there are two places to normally cross.

In the dank dawn, I walked under the eerie pine trees of Bellever Forest and out along the Lych Way. Bellever Forest always seemed creepy in the dark and knowing that you were on the old road they used to carry coffins along certainly didn't help the atmosphere. I passed through the forest.

There are two main places to cross the East Dart River: at Waterfall or at Sandy Hole Pass. Excluding, of course, walking all the way round the source or crossing on the road through Postbridge. One is slightly further upstream than the other. Both are due north of the ridge of tors I needed to access in the later part of the day.

Although the Lych Way had been resurfaced recently, to reclaim it from a particularly voracious bog, a herd of cows had decided they'd prefer to stand on the path than get their feet wet. Who knew if there were calves in the fog. I cut straight across the bog to Arch Tor to avoid their dark shapes. My feet were already too wet to notice.

Waterfall is the lower of the two crossings, the closest to Postbridge. The river drops down through a narrow gap between two large boulders. The rocks are big enough that you can walk easily across their wide flat tops, with maybe very shallow puddles spilling out across them, and a small step over the river in between. It's an easy way to get to Lower White Tor and beyond.

Arch Tor successfully bagged, I clomped back through the bog, back along the Lych Way and into Postbridge. It was empty, but I arrived at the same time as the guy who unlocks the Visitor Centre toilets. Success. After a quick stop, I headed out north across the field to reach a set of tors on the east side of the East Dart. A notoriously wet field on the best of days, the river had spilled its banks at the bottom corner. I sploshed on by.

Sandy Hole Pass is further up river from Waterfall. The crossing point is at the start of a narrow, straight gorge, artificially straightened by medieval tin miners. You can hop across large round boulders, smooth like enormous pebbles, or jump across inside the pass itself. Less straightforward than Waterfall and less direct, but still a good option.

Four tors down for the day, I crouched behind one of Sittaford Tor's many adjoining walls. One of them is always out of the wind. Sort of. It was more windy than foggy now. I could see a good couple of hundred metres around the tor. But there was still a cloud of persistent drizzle hanging over everything.

I shrugged off my rucksack and sat on a rock between some reeds. It was good to be out of the wind for a bit. The weather created a strange sort of clammy damp. The sneaky kind of rain that you don't really notice until everything is soaked. At first you're not sure if you're damp from the inside or the outside. I wiped the layer of moisture off my face, somewhat unsuccessfully, with a damp glove.

There was a red light flashing out of the top of my rucksack. It was the tracker: low battery. Great. The battery was meant to last weeks, but I'd borrowed it and just assumed the batteries would be fresh. Maybe they were, the weather probably wasn't helping. I had some spares but it was too wet to try to replace them now. Perhaps the live tracking map was showing how much battery I had left? For all I knew red flashing light could mean days of battery left – or minutes. I dropped a text to Mum and Dad to see if they could tell.

Behind me, the water was pouring down off the hills. Dartmoor had reached saturation point. Dartmoor is naturally boggy: under its grassy shell is a layer of peat and then impermeable granite. Now the bog was full of water it had nowhere else to go. Water cascaded out of every dip in the grass and off downhill. My feet were swimming.

Leaving Sittaford Tor, I climbed carefully over the slippery wooden stile. They always had about as much grip as an ice rink in these conditions. Face south, follow wall, two kilometres to the river. Waterfall or Sandy Hole Pass? Soon we'd find out.

I heard the river before I could see it: loud as the wind, louder, but in a lower and continuous roar. Through the mist, I looked down on a raging torrent of a river, crashing down off the moor. I'd considered where the wall crossed the river as a desperate third option for crossing. You might be able to shimmy across holding onto the wood and wire, I'd thought. No chance. The fence was underwater. It looked like the kind of place where sheep go to die. The crossing was way too wide and you'd quickly get sucked under and trapped in the wire mesh.

Next crossing point. I turned and walked up river. It looked powerful. At least twice as wide as I could jump and thundering down its channel as if running very late for an appointment in Postbridge. The water was a murky brown colour, the same shade as I was wringing out of my socks most nights. But on top were bold white crests of froth and foam.

I reached Waterfall and laughed at my own stupidity.

There was no way I could cross here. The river wasn't trickling through a gap, it was ignoring the gap altogether and plunging straight over the drop. The sheer volume of rain we'd had in the last week should have been a clue. Both rocks, usually high above the river, were a foot under. The river was too wide to jump and you don't want to be wading out in a fast river above a drop. Nope. It would have to be Sandy Hole Pass.

Further up the river I trudged. In some places it looked narrow enough that I might be able to make it across. Maybe if my bag wasn't so heavy. Maybe I could throw my bag across first? Fine unless I couldn't get across after it. I didn't fancy being stuck on the wrong side of a river to everything keeping me alive. And if either of us missed the far bank, that would be disaster.

Staying close to the river, but not too close, I clambered along the bank until I reached Sandy Hole Pass. Or at least where the crossing at Sandy Hole Pass should have been. I couldn't see it. There was the place where the banks rose up either side of the river. But there were no boulders to be seen. The water was flat and fast out the channel. I stopped and simply stared at the river. Now what? I'd never seen it so high.

What do you do when you can't cross a river? You walk upstream.

"I'll just go a little further and see."

So I walked, up and up, water always to my left and a haze of grey to my right. I clambered up the slope of Sandy Hole Pass and walked above the straight channel, as close to the river as I dared. It was narrower here. Narrow but deep. Fast and deep. Could I jump it? Maybe just. It would be hard to land properly on the far bank. No flat patch to run it off – I'd face plant into the slope or land in the clitter and topple backwards.

How fast was it going? That was always a key point in swift water safety lectures. They say you can judge a river based on its speed: walking pace, running pace... At running pace you shouldn't cross. No leisurely jogs for this river. The East Dart was sprinting. I thought of all the crossing techniques taught to Mountain Leaders, the techniques that seem bonkers when you're demonstrating to a group in ankle deep water. But they were emergency techniques and ones that rely on having a lot of people to hand. There was no one here to help prop me upright against the force of this river.

I sighed, "I'll just go a little further."

By 12:30 pm, an hour after I'd reached the river, I was wading through Broad Marsh. There was still nowhere to cross. Red and white range poles appeared out of the mist. They were firing today. I was stuck.

Instead of getting narrower, the whole river had swelled out into the bog. I supposed I probably could have guessed that. It felt like I was walking on a leaky waterbed. The bog oozed out murky water with every step, often forcing a hasty retreat and wider berth around, taking me out of view of the river. This was no good. I walked uphill away from the river, far enough to find a patch of ground less damp than I was to sit on. I threw my bag down, sat on it and put my head in my hands. What should I do now?

Devastated, I pulled out a wrap and started to munch. I chewed and stared like a sheep munches on grass, blank-eyed and absent. When the wrap was gone, I wrung out each of my gloves and put them back on again. Then I took another wrap.

I stared down at the river. I'd been pushed into a corner. On one side was the firing range. Yeah, I could just sneak into the range, cross the river and sneak back again. But who knew how far up river I'd have to walk to cross. It was still another four kilometres to the source. And anyway, walking into a live firing range in the fog is beyond my level of reckless. I could literally get shot.

Somehow I had to cross this river, but everything I'd seen of it was awful. I imagined my little tracker dot flashing on the empty map page. Tiny and alone. I pictured people watching it with baited breath. They'd see the range markers on the map. They'd guess the river would be high. What's she going to do next?

What *is* she going to do next? Maybe I could go down here and jump across it. My imaginary audience gasped, holding their collective breath in suspense before the leap and then – success, cheering! She made it! But there was the other outcome. The miss, the slip, the toppling backwards into a fast river without anyone to pull me out. No one to save me. The audience shrieked and cried. Er, what? I withdrew from the imaginary people in my head. That was a bit over the top. This isn't a game show. You lot can go away now.

Who was really watching? I thought about my parents. If anyone in the world was watching, it was them. I thought about what Steve had said last night. There were people watching, even if they weren't watching very hard. And they did care. I couldn't risk falling in the river. There was only one horrendous option left.

The only choice was to walk the six kilometres back to Postbridge, cross the river via the road and then walk all the way back up the other side. It was the safest and most soul destroying option. I finished my wrap and put my head in my hands. My hair was wet, my hat was wet, my gloves were wet. I just wanted to curl up and hide from the onslaught. The weather, the bad luck – everything.

Years ago, when I was a teenager, my 45 team had tried to beat the Ten Tors speed record on a training weekend. We'd met the leaders close to nightfall on day one, some thirty miles in. I was shattered, exhausted, with a blister under every toe. Apparently I'd looked broken too.

"Do you feel like you've got the record in you?" Stu had asked me.

"No," I'd said. "But I'm going to do it anyway."

I stood up, saddled up my pack and squelched back towards civilisation.

CHAPTER 12 – PEOPLE

I arrived at Postbridge in a cloud of fury. How could I have been so stupid? Why didn't I turn back sooner? I'd walked miles past Lower White Tor on the east bank of the river. It was obvious by the wall that the river was too high. There was no way I was going to be able to cross. I should have made the call earlier and saved myself the extra miles and time and struggle.

The path back to Postbridge is long and straight and I knew it backwards, even in the fog. Sure it was narrow in places, with gorse bushes and deep mud, but what did I care? I shoved past the spikes and powered through the mud. If I'd wasted all this time on the river, I was certainly going to undo the mess as quickly as possible. I passed a DofE group, slightly higher up the hill, probably looking for the path. It was much lower than the green dashed line marked on the map. Probably pretty bemused to watch me storm past below them, but I didn't care. I was wrapped up in my own little bubble of rage that carried me all the way back to the Visitor Centre at Postbridge.

Five hours, four tors and I was back where I started. Almost. I threw my bag down under the awning behind the public toilets and exhaled.

"Right. We're back at Postbridge."

Next stop, Higher White Tor. Lower White wasn't even worth stopping at. I peeled off my waterproof jacket and put another fleece on underneath, tucking it into my waterproof trousers. Making the most of the shelter and the bench, I ate a pack of oatcakes and shifted some fruit leathers into easy access pockets. Then I pulled on a damp hat and damp gloves, yanked my hood up and headed back out into the rain.

Crossing the car park, I slipped through the gap in the wall and onto the path that runs back out along the west bank of the East Dart. It was fairly sheltered for now, a narrow lane sandwiched between two field walls. At the final gate, I chose the higher path and plodded back out into the open moors. There were still seven tors to do today. Here we go again.

Little did I know what was going on outside my personal battle with the elements. A day or so later I received a text from Mark, another Dartmoor Rescue friend. He'd spent two hours sitting on Higher White Tor waiting for me, just the other side of the river, while I paced up and down the bank. It was not sitting around weather and eventually the wind and the rain had won. He'd given up and gone home.

Andy told me weeks later that my tracker had frozen somewhere between Sandy Hole Pass and the firing range boundary. He had a tab open on his computer at work and kept checking the map. I wasn't moving. He thought I'd gone in. He was almost at the point of considering an unofficial rescue mission when the trace had lurched back into life and placed me in Postbridge.

Meanwhile, on Dartmoor, I felt like the entire world had been rubbed out. It was just me and a hundred metre circle of bog. I imagined myself from a distance: a bright red speck in a moving patch of brown, like a spotlight, in an empty white-grey universe. Nothing else existed. The rucksack weighed down on my shoulders. My hips chafed under the waist belt, pinched under so many layers of overlapping clothing. It rained into my face, with a desultory slap in the gusts. I pulled my hood down as far as I could against the assault, just enough to still be able to see. Then I started singing quietly to myself, mumbling as I stumbled forwards against the weather.

When I gained the ridge, the wind was gusting so hard it almost knocked me over. Rucksack and all. I picked off Lower White Tor without stopping and made straight for Higher White. There wasn't much shelter. More food. More water. I carried on.

As I pushed down the ridge through Longaford Tor, Littaford, Crocken – another 'easy' ridgeline on the plan – my mind drifted away from the present. I thought of other times I'd walked this ridgeline, warmer times, drier times, pleasant jaunts with friends and family. Then of my first find with Dartmoor Rescue. In the calm silence of the night, my torch had swept across a tor. Instead of rocks it had found a shoulder, then a face. I don't think I'll ever forget it.

You're only ever an inch away from disaster. You just don't know what's coming. One tiny misjudgement, one step out of place. It's accidents or crossing the road that will get you, not the apocalypse. I know this. Yet it's always tempting to push the boundary a little bit further. A bad thing could happen, but it won't actually happen to me. I'll be alright. Until it's not alright. Until suddenly a compound of tiny poor decisions tips you over into the realms of real danger.

I almost tried to jump that river. I almost gave in to the voice in my head that said everything would be alright. I might have made it. But if I hadn't… What exactly was completing this challenge worth to me? Not that. Things could have got very bad very quickly. With this bag on, I would have been sucked down deep with the water and that would have been me, lying dead in a river. Maybe I would have knocked my head on a rock. Or been pulled under with my rucksack and swept downstream until I tumbled over Waterfall. I guess eventually someone would have noticed there was something odd about my tracking map.

But what shook me most was that I needed other people to make that good decision: to turn and go back. It was thinking of them that had made me do it. I couldn't do it independently.

There wasn't anyone there to question my ideas or point out that throwing myself across a river in spate was, on the face of it, completely mad. It's easy to see the right choice when you're in a group or taking care of others. I tend to make more sensible decisions with an added leadership responsibility, or company. But actually, even when you're alone, you're still looking after someone. You're looking after the lives of the people who aren't there with you. The people you've left behind who want everything to turn out alright.

CHAPTER 13 – STRAWBERRIES

The day was nearly over. I walked down the end of the track into Two Bridges, trying to avoid the dog poo. That was the last thing I wanted to deal with right now. The ditches either side of the path were full of water. My waterproofs had taken on a glossy sheen, no longer repelling the rain in bead-like droplets. Rain dripped off my hood, onto my cheeks and down my sleeves every time I moved. There was a slow, warm seep of damp soaking up my trousers from my socks. I was warm enough, but only by moving. The cold would get me very quickly if I stopped.

I hoped they'd be there. "Would be good to bump into you at Two Bridges" was pretty cryptic as text messages go, but I hadn't had a chance to see if they'd replied. Perhaps I could check when I got to the car park. I really didn't want to stand in the rain getting cold. It would be dark soon.

As I reached the end of the track, the normally busy car

park looked empty. Not really the day for an evening jaunt to Wistman's Wood. Dismal, I unlatched the gate and then I saw it: a battered, red people carrier tucked into the far corner. The car we'd had almost all my life. The only car in the car park.

Dad was in the driver's seat, wrapped up in several fleeces. Mum was in the seat next to him, all scarves and blankets. They had the engine off, hunkering down against the storm. I walked over but they were both looking away, down at Mum's phone, trying to get something to work. I stood in front of the window and waved. Mum glanced up and caught sight of the dark shape in front of the window. But as soon as she realised this bedraggled creature was her daughter, her startled face warmed into a big grin.

They cracked open a door, "Hello! Wait a minute, we'll open up the back."

I propped my bag up against the back of the car and stood with it under the open boot.

"It's freezing. Want to come in?"

"I'm soaked."

"Wait a minute, we'll get the..." Mum started to pull an old tarp out of the stowage box and laid it out in the empty back of the car. With all the seats removed, there was a lot of space. I grabbed the tracker out of my bag and climbed onto the tarp. Dad shut the boot behind me.

"Oh, yes, your tracker, we brought spare batteries."

Mum got back out of the passenger seat, opened a side door and started rummaging through some shopping bags. She found something and pulled it out.

"I brought you strawberries!"

She held out the punnet towards me, smiling.

My waterproofs were making a large puddle on the tarp. I was at a loss what to say.

"Thank you."

She put them down beyond the edge of the puddle and carried on rifling through the bags until she found the spare batteries.

"There you go."

As soon as she shut the door, Dad put the heating on. "We saw you had some trouble crossing the river."

"Yeah it was too high and they're firing in Merrivale today, so I had to go all the way back to Postbridge."

I picked up the batteries and the tracker. "Do you have something flat? A small coin? A paper clip…?"

"Erm…"

It was the kind of car that accumulated stuff, from mints and sunglasses to a bag of marbles that had somehow never belonged anywhere else. But apparently nothing small and flat.

"Don't worry, I'm just… I'll get my penknife." I pulled it out the pile of wet clothes and started unscrewing the back of the tracker.

"So how have you been?"

We talked over the journey so far, through all the twists and turns. Mum and Dad asked me about particular details they'd seen on my trace. A lot had happened in six days.

"Mum," I said eventually, "did you get the strawberries especially for me? Like as a treat?"

"Oh no, I just wanted to make sure I had something in case you were hungry."

"I am hungry," I agreed, "but I think I had better eat something hot. What time is it?"

"It's about half five."

"Already!" I'd got there at 5 o'clock, "Well, maybe I'll eat dinner down here and then carry on for the last two tors. It's going to be really hard to light a stove up there in this weather."

The more I thought about it, the more it seemed like a great idea.

"Okay, sure."

"Can I cook in the car?"

They swapped uncertain glances.

"Let's just find something in case it spills," said Dad.

"It won't spill," I said, sitting on an enormous tarp.

"Hang on, we'll find..."

"Don't worry, I'll do it outside. I'm just being lazy. Can you open the boot?"

Dad opened the boot and I slid myself back out, braced against the weather. I shook my waterproof jacket out, then put it back on and rummaged in my bag to find the stove and food. Behind the back wheel of the car seemed to be the place most out of the wind. I set up and stared at the stove until it boiled. Then I grabbed a ration pack and spoon and carried the pan into the car, pulling the door shut behind me.

I poured the water into my dehydrated chilli and sat holding it like a hot water bottle. It is the longest wait in the world, waiting 15 ravenous minutes for your dinner to rehydrate. I usually save a mini pack of biscuits to fill the gap, but today's were long gone.

Finally, my chilli was ready and I shovelled down the warm food gladly. Soon everything felt much better. We talked some more. Eventually, it was really time to head off. I'd been there almost an hour.

"Right, well I should probably go soon. I want to find a place to camp before it gets very dark." It was almost 6 o'clock already and Dartmoor's characteristic misty gloom was starting to set in.

"Where are you going next?"

"I'm going to go up through the farm to Beardown, the way we used to go on Ten Tors. Then I'll follow the range poles up to Crow Tor. Hopefully there'll be somewhere I can camp out of the wind."

"Do we know Crow Tor?" asked Mum, looking at Dad.

"Yeah, Dad and I spent hours looking for a letterbox up there once."

I was about nine years old. It was just one time, back when I was on a quest to join the 100 Club. There's no way they were going to remember it.

"Anyway," I continued, "thanks for the batteries and everything – and the use of your back wheel!"

I started packing up and stood next to the car, ready to head off. Mum was wearing a face reserved for train stations and airport departures, but I barely noticed. I was already thinking ahead into the night: the route, the camp.

"I can hug you if you like, but you'll get wet."

As I climbed onto the stile into the woods, I heard the

familiar rev of the car's engine. I turned and waved. Mum was peering out the window but I don't think they saw me against the forest. The lights passed. Quietly, I slipped between the trees.

CHAPTER 14 – CIVILISATION

There was something wrong with the tent. It looked… odd. I sat up in my sleeping bag. Definitely odd. Packing up inside, I opened the porch to put my dry sleeping kit into my rucksack. On top of the bag, outside of the porch, rested something huge, like an ominous bulge in a marquee roof. Ah. I poked it. Ah. I zipped the tent back up, working up the motivation to pull on my soggy wet walking trousers from where they'd spent the night bunched up at the bottom of the tent. Yum – and completely self inflicted.

The night before, I'd arrived well after dark and pitched in a hurry. It turned out that Crow Tor was much lumpier than I remembered: all grassed-over rocks and a small stack, providing almost no shelter from the wind. In fact, the tor is angled in such a way that it looks like it's sliding down the hill. I'd wandered back down the slope until I'd found something passable. It was too cold to be picky.

Eager to get moving as soon as possible, now there was clammy wet fabric stuck to my legs, I put feet into boots and launched myself out of the tent. The fresh morning sky rose to greet me: it wasn't raining. There might even be some blue sky coming later. Turning back around, I caught sight of the tent and burst into fits of laughter. There was an enormous puddle resting across one side of the tent. The resulting impression was as if it had been pitched by a Bronze DofE group and then sat on. To me, it was hilarious. In fact, it was so hilarious, I had to take a picture before I dismantled anything. At least this was conclusive evidence that the tent was indeed waterproof.

A gust of wind set my legs shivering.

"Right then, time to go."

I dismantled my train-wreck of a tent and set off into deepest darkest Dartmoor. Today I was heading out north to Fur Tor before a U-turn back towards civilisation. The wind was up, but not bad. My trousers got a brisk blow dry. The clouds were becoming small and distant. A rainbow arced overhead as I merrily squelched along beside the range poles. This was the life.

I ticked off a row of tors, including the oxymoronic Flat Tor, as underwhelming as promised. Either the tor had sunk or the grass had risen to cover most of it. A small leap over Cut Hill Water, at the very top end of the East Dart, and I headed up the peat pass to Fur Tor.

Fur Tor, as any good pub quiz will tell you, is the Dartmoor tor that's furthest from any road. It had taken me years to make the pilgrimage. Fur Tor wasn't on any of the routes I normally took, nor particularly close to anything else. It had required a special trip. This time it felt just as special. The view was a sight for sore eyes. It swooped down towards Tavy Cleave and spread out wide across the North Moor. Dappled light crossed the moorland below through gaps in the clouds above. The undulating grass stretched out in all directions, in pastel shades of brown and orange and ochre, mottled like a Widgery painting. There was not a soul in sight: just me and Dartmoor.

But there was much more tor bagging to be done today. I turned and headed south, back across miles of wide boggy plain. Most of West Devon's rivers start in this square kilometre of bog; the spring in my step wasn't just from the mild weather. There was nothing up here, just rolling plains of peat and grass. No sheep or birds or people: desolate. I walked south in a vast silence, punctuated by the uncanny sound of machine gun fire. I knew they weren't firing in the range I was in, but it still made you want to duck and run for cover.

Devil's Tor, Conies Down Tor and Lydford Tor flew by. It was all so easy today. The entire North Moor complete, I headed for the end of the road at Holming Beam. I needed to cross through Princetown again to reach the rest of today's tors.

As I reached the car park, I could see a large white van driving fast down the long straight road towards me. Either I was about to have a very strange encounter, or… well, there was one person it could be.

The van swung across the empty car park, filling it, and

a window rolled down. It was Huck.

"Emm! Made it! Thought I was going to miss you."

Huck runs his family's removal company. He was out on a job, having lunch in Princetown, when he spotted I was nearby.

"You were going so fast I wasn't sure I'd catch you. I brought you something."

He got out of the cab and proffered a huge slab of cake on a white napkin.

"Thank you!" I took it and started to pick at the icing. "How did the Plodders open evening go last night?"

"Seriously? You're out here, doing this and thinking about that?"

I shrugged, "I've got to think about something."

"Yeah, it went well, some new kids showed up too so that's all good. Should have plenty for teams next year. I told all the kids and parents about what you're doing."

"Oh!" I was surprised. "Thanks."

"They love it. Some of them have decided they want to do all the tors too. How's it been?"

"Grim," I grinned. "Rubbish weather, no sleep, six ticks and I'm getting some pretty interesting chafing on my legs from wet trousers… Oh and I got charged by a bull below Watern."

"Feet?"

"Fine. Blister on the balls of each foot and one on my left heel. Right one's popped. The trouble's the wet really – they don't get long enough to dry out."

My blisters had been legendary while I was doing Ten

Tors. So legendary, in fact, that the local outdoor shop asked for a photo to use as a point of reference for customers complaining of 'bad' blisters.

Before long, Huck had to get back to work, "I'm sorry I can't make the finish on Tuesday – I've got another job on."

"Oh gosh, no worries at all."

I honestly didn't expect anyone to come to the finish. By this stage, I rather imagined quietly crawling back onto the bench in Princetown square, unannounced, and calling it a day. We were talking about only four days' time, but the end still seemed so far away. There was a lot of walking to do. I strolled down Holming Beam, cake in one hand, waving with the other, until the van disappeared out of sight. The cake was gone before I reached the end of the road.

After crossing pleasantly cow-free fields, I arrived in Princetown. Reaching the Fox Tor Cafe, I immediately walked straight round the back, dumped my bag neatly down by the pond and sat down on a damp picnic bench. My body was on autopilot.

The Fox Tor Cafe is a proper walkers' caff – a place packed full of noisy people and muddy walking boots, windows so steamy you can't see inside. They keep the fire roaring, love your dog and serve all day breakfast. Almost every Dartmoor Plodders walk ends in the Fox Tor Cafe and has done for as long as I've been around. In fact, as a one-time walker myself, I've been accidentally conditioned into feeling that – whatever the current owner may think – I actually, secretly, own the place. After all, the Plodders have outlived generations of owners. Through all sorts of menus and décor, we've always finished our walks here and always had our Ten Tors podium photos displayed on the back wall. Legend has it that they built the cafe around our photos.

Sitting out the back, I went completely unnoticed. I guess you might say I was part of the furniture. Although when half the furniture has been painted a luminous Plodders green, perhaps that's cause to worry. I unrolled my phone from its waterproof sandwich bag and turned it on. I was keeping it off mostly to save the battery. Stifling the polyphonic ringtone into my leg, I waited as 18 text messages came through, one after another. That was pretty much my year's quota of texts in one day.

Of course, 18 texts in a year doesn't include messages from SARCALL, the automated bot that alerts Dartmoor Rescue to callouts. I have a long running joke with Steve that I get all my texts from this guy called SARCALL.

"Yeah," I'd laugh, "we don't chat much but when he calls I always come running."

Slowly, I flipped through the text messages. They were all from friends and family wishing me well on the moors. Not, of course, that they were 18 full individual messages. I am the proud owner of an old-school Nokia brick that splits incoming texts into 160 character chunks, the height of tech in 2001. I'd got it second hand from my cousin 14 years ago and it was still going strong. Not the flashiest, but hell is it a survivor.

Still, what I read made me smile. Messages dealt with, I went into the porter cabin to use the toilets and fill up my water. As a regular patron for over a decade, I didn't think Dave would mind. Of course it would have been an excellent excuse to buy a bowl of chips, but I hadn't brought any money. Not even a card.

The Fox Tor Cafe is famous for its breakfasts. The leaders often had them, sitting and waiting for the teams to come in at the end of a long weekend. Stu would buy you breakfast if you beat the Ten Tors record. It was the only time I'd ever eaten one and that had somehow made it sacred. Still, I am a huge advocate of their sausage and egg baps. You can't beat a large bowl of chips when you're cold and wet, nor find a better hot chocolate on Dartmoor.

One year, I'd invited some university friends down for a camping trip. Of course, I had to take them to the Fox Tor Cafe as part of the full Dartmoor experience. It was a scorching summer's day, so we'd found a picnic bench out the back in the shade. I ordered a bowl of chips, but they both decided that they wanted to cool off with a fresh bowl of salad.

The full Fox Tor Cafe experience does not involve salad. There wasn't a single salad on the menu. The waiter was baffled. No one had ever tried to order a salad before. I apologised profusely, feeling like my friends had somewhat missed the point. Particularly when they didn't think much of the salad that arrived.

In fact, it was these same friends who'd stood on top of Cox Tor and exclaimed, "What, you mean you haven't been to all of them?"

As if visiting all the tors was somehow a prerequisite to

being from Dartmoor. I'd started to explain the complexities of the concepts 'tor' and 'all' but thought better of it. What did they really care anyway? They wouldn't get it.

Back out on the road through Princetown, I did some calculations. It was only 2 o'clock and with just a couple of tors left, I could easily get ahead of schedule. If I was going to do that, I needed to check where the wild camping boundaries were exactly. They're a bit intricate around Princetown because of private land and the Burrator catchment area.

I walked into the Dartmoor Visitor Centre expecting some sort of fanfare. Nothing happened. I walked over to the counter and smiled at the lady behind it.

"How can I help you?" she asked, no sign of recognition. Perhaps lots of people in muddy boots and gaiters come in carrying huge backpacks each day.

"I'm your Love Moor Life Ambassador," I began.

"Yes, I know who you are."

Oh. Right. Then why aren't you surprised to see me? Although this lady did seem like the kind of person who would be unfazed whoever walked up to the counter, be it the Queen or Elvis.

"I was wondering if you had a copy of the camping map that I could take?"

She pulled the correct leaflet out from the selection behind her desk.

"How did it go?"

"How did what go?"

"Your big walk – all the tors."

"Ohhhhh, I'm sorry, I see why we're at odds here. I'm still doing it! I'm just over halfway through."

"I see. You look remarkably fresh for it."

"Oh," I said, knowing I was probably the grubbiest I'd been in my life. Perhaps all this rain counted as having a shower. "Thank you. I'm a bit ahead of schedule so I just wanted to check the wild camping boundaries. I didn't think to mark them on my map."

"When do you finish?"

"Tuesday morning, hopefully."

"I don't work on Tuesdays, but good luck."

Outside, I consulted the camping leaflet. In the direction I was going, the boundaries were actually quite simple. I just had to make sure I walked far enough tonight to be inside them. Strategy decided, I left Princetown to tackle the South Moor.

CHAPTER 15 – PARANOIA

I sat on Bench Tor and cried. Tiny tears of desperation crept down my face in silence. I was too exhausted to keep them back. The lack of sleep was really starting to catch up with me.

Last night I'd managed one tor extra and a few more miles before stopping to make camp. I couldn't force myself any further. The flats of my feet were killing me. Finding a level square of grass where I could pitch my tent out of the wind made it worth it. I had so many memories of miserable wet evenings in this part of the moor. Most of the grass was the kind you walked through, not on.

Everything was going smoothly until it started to rain. I ducked into the tent, managing to kick over a pan of freshly boiled water as I went. Give me a break. At least it didn't spill inside the tent. But even such a small inconvenience caused an outburst of frustration and despair. I was at the end of frayed nerves. Sure, I was ahead now, but every inch was hard won. Nothing could be easy.

Chewing on mushroom risotto the consistency of warm playdough, I thought about the route ahead. I didn't look at the map. The tors were becoming few and far between and I knew what was coming. Soon I would reach the section I'd been dreading the entire walk.

When you're trying to join the dots between 119 tors, you try to be nice to yourself. You start with the obvious bits: ridgelines, paths, the bits you know from Ten Tors – or just from life. Then you try to connect those sections together sensibly… and so it goes on until you're left with two ends that need joining. My two ends were Bench Tor and Shipley Tor. There was no obvious – or even sensible – way to cross the eight or so kilometres between them. The way was a mess of enclosures, dry leats, tin workings and field boundaries. No paths or even flat ground. I couldn't find a way, so I'd simply taken a ruler and joined the dots. I'll work it out when I get there.

That night, I fell asleep praying for another clear day. I still had no idea how to make that crossing. If I didn't have the weather on side, it would be a disaster. I just wanted to be able to see. Was that so much to ask?

The next morning I was there, staring at it. Or, more specifically, at a grey wall of fog 30 metres in front of me. This was it. I had banked on clear weather. I was screwed. I had no idea where to even start, so I simply sat on Bench Tor, desperately facing the first step. Dartmoor couldn't keep it together either. It was raining and getting harder.

Hiding the camera inside a heavy duty drybag, I told it my woes.

"Okay, I'm on Bench Tor... It's raining too hard to let you out the bag..."

I adjusted the bag.

"Um, I'm... I'm at Bench Tor. I have to get to Shipley Tor... Which is kind of the other side of Dartmoor... Near Shipley Bridge... funnily enough."

I rolled my eyes at myself. Really, Emily?

"... and I've never walked that way before, it's really not obvious – and of course, it's foggy so I can't see more than 30 metres, maybe 50 metres maximum. I don't know which way to go. I'm really tired so I'm already making stupid navigational decisions this morning..."

I sighed. I'd tried to go the clearly wrong way around Venford Reservoir, choosing a steep wooded valley and a river crossing instead of a large stone bridge. I'd taken one look at the valley and walked all the way back round again.

"... and I just want to get on a path and put my head down and walk! But I can't... I have to... I have to navigate. In the fog... And I don't know which is the best way to go really..."

There was nothing more to say. I put the camera away and just stared out at the moor. Vast black shapes moved in the mist around me. The cows were closing in, I needed to move on.

Right. Navigate. Break it down. Let's give this a shot.

I took a bearing and paced 600 metres back to Venford Reservoir dam.

Okay, now follow the road until the corner. It's not a

sharp bend. It won't be obvious. Pace it: 400 metres.

Then what? I wanted to take a bearing to a specific point. Anything distinct within a kilometre. Maybe an enclosure? They're not always there. The cairns? A kink in the leat? There wasn't anything bigger. But it was all irrelevant because, when I reached the bend in the road, there was a wall of gorse bushes in the way.

I paced another 50 metres along the road, looking for an opening. One hundred metres... argh just let me in already! If I kept following this road I'd end up in Ashburton.

Finally, I found a gap and pushed through onto the grass. Okay. Bearing. Let's try to find this enclosure.

It became very apparent very quickly that any exact bearings would be hard to follow. The moor here was a maze of tiny paths, barely the width of a rucksack, winding between dense gorse bushes. Try to walk in a straight line and be impaled on a thousand tiny green spears.

By this point, I knew that all the cows were out to get me. Every single one had a personal vendetta against me. And they were everywhere. As I navigated through the maze of spikes, I did my best to avoid them. But they kept sneaking up on me. They were closing in from all sides like a sinister, live action version of Pac-Man, with the speed turned right down. Ghostly cows slowly appeared out of the fog, coming to eat you unless you could find another path. Don't let them get too close or you might get trapped. It didn't help that the cows at the edge of the fog kept turning into gorse bushes as I approached. How was I supposed to know which path was safe?

The gorse bush labyrinth spat me out at the corner of a drystone wall. One part headed off downhill, the other contoured round. I'd lost count of my exact pacing. If you're not walking in a straight line, you're only really counting to stay awake. So I stood at the corner and tried to relocate. Normally it would be a two second job. You'd just take a bearing along the direction of the wall and line it up with the walls on the map – but the fog and the gorse bushes conspired against me.

"I just need to go down and check," I told no one in particular.

A little way down the wall I got close enough to take a good bearing along it. I put the compass on my map and tried to find a match.

"That one... or that one. No, too steep. It's probably this one."

Decision made, I headed back uphill and stood at the corner again. I looked up at the walls, down at the map, back up at the wall and jumped out of my skin. The cow-sized space between me and the wall corner was now filled with a cow. It was bulbous and brown and so close I could have touched it. A pair of wide, dark eyes fixed me in a cold stare.

Terrified, I backed away slowly, careful not to trip up on the tussock grass. How did it get there? I couldn't take my eyes off the cow in case it attacked. It might charge if I turned my back on it. The cow remained still. I kept reversing. Where had it come from? Were there more? Was this a decoy from the rest of the pack?

I edged anxiously away and around it through the scrub

until I had no option. I turned my back and sprint-staggered 30 metres along the upper wall until the cow would be lost in the fog. Panting, I walked another 100 metres or so to be sure I was safe. Then, checking there weren't more cows out hunting, I sat down.

Collapsed on the grass, I wiped the rain water off the map and stared at it. The map gave me no answers. There was nothing to go off – not unless I handrailed round the erratic doodle of wall boundaries at the edge of the moor. Even in my wrecked state I was so not up for that. I just needed to cover ground and get out of this mess. At least I seemed to be out of the Gorse Maze of Doom now. I peered deeper into the map.

Wait. Cows! Check for cows! In momentary panic, I dropped the map and braced to spring up or defend myself. I scoured the fog line. No cows.

Then I had an idea. I'd drawn a straight line on the planning map, so that's what I should do now. I'd just walk in a straight line. If I set a bearing to south west and kept the wall on my left and the slope to my right I could at least get to Pupers, or Snowdon, or somewhere. This seemed like as sound a plan as any. There wasn't really a catching feature if I missed the landmarks in the fog, but oh well.

I set the compass and started walking. Every little while I'd stop and check I was still going in the right direction. It seemed to be working. The slope was mostly clear, with normal sized bracken, turning brown and limp with old age. An odd stumpy hawthorn appeared here or there, a bush, a few rocks. No cows. There was an impression through the bracken that I was sort of able to follow like a path.

I was still moving forwards when I looked down at my compass and casually thought, "That's funny, south west wasn't in that direction a minute ago."

It was a few moments before the full gravity of that statement sunk in. I stopped walking and examined the compass. For some time – although I'd no idea how long – I'd been walking south east. Right.

I wasn't counting my paces any more. I'd caught myself stuck in an infinite loop of '48… 49… 40… 41…' Unsure of how long I'd been there, I simply let the numbers go.

Adjusting the bearing back to south west, I stared at the compass intently and made sure to get the red needle between the two white lines. But it was already starting to feel a bit futile. I could be basically anywhere. My brain had reached breaking point. My compass hand dropped to my side. I couldn't force myself to navigate any more, so I just walked.

Eventually, I came across a boundary stone, small enough that you could trip over it in the fog. But it was there and it was real: a squat lump of granite engraved with a big letter H.

"Aha," I thought. "This must be on the map."

The stone was in the bottom of a dip, grassy on both sides with reeds and bog in the middle. Not distinguishing features really. It could have been a river, or it could have been a path. Everything was so soaked there was no way of telling the difference.

Pulling out my map, I examined the part I hoped I was

on, scanning for the friendly letters BS for Boundary Stone. There was nothing. I widened my search by a kilometre and found two. But neither fitted the lay of the land that I could see. Either I was unbelievably lost or the boundary stone wasn't on the map. It happens. But it didn't look like a new stone.

H is not a common letter for a boundary stone. Most that have inscriptions are carved with two or three letters, the initials of places or boundaries that they mark the ancient lines between. Hapstead Ford was marked on the map and not outside the realms of possibility for where I could be. Although perhaps anything was possible now. It was in a narrow channel with a river running through it. I liked that idea. The more I looked, the more it seemed like the only answer. It had to be true. I was either there or I was very, very lost. I must be at Hapstead Ford.

Tucking that fact up my sleeve, I returned to the map with new purpose. Okay, if that's true, where do I need to go now? South. Walk south for four kilometres until you fall into Avon Dam Reservoir. Perfect. I didn't even need a bearing for that.

The mist had eaten all of Dartmoor. It had eaten any sense of the passage of time or distance or direction. Now it was going to eat me. I was off on a journey to wherever the black compass needle would take me. Resigned to my fate, I set off into the mist until it swallowed me too.

CHAPTER 16 – WET

Tarmac. My feet pounded on it. My socks squelched. It was a bitter-sweet sensation, pain crossed with relief. No more tripping over tussocks, I barely had to lift my feet above its smooth surface. But it was extra hard on my tender feet. My boots never got a chance to dry out any more. I wonder how you get trench foot? Someone had said I would get trench foot.

By fluke or providence I had found my way to Avon Dam, an unmistakable reservoir. When I'd first joined the Plodders they'd told me there were whales in it. No whales today, but a long straight path from the east bank all the way to Shipley Tor. Now this was a double dashed track. It was a sandy brown groove across the hillside, keeping close to the water. Then all of a sudden, the track turned into a road. I couldn't believe it. It seemed so out of place. I took a delicate first step onto the tarmac, in case it wasn't real. It felt so wrong – and the wrongness continued.

The mist had started to lift as the rain got harder. The moor I saw around me looked foreign. There were so many plants. To get up to Shipley Tor, I needed to go through it. I bashed my way off the road through bracken and rhododendron and… plants. This was not my Dartmoor.

Right up until the last minute, the cows were trying to thwart me. I waded through the undergrowth, surrounded by signs that the cows had been there. The plants were trampled flat as if a whole herd of monsters had lain there for the night. I was acutely aware that I was using their tracks to get through this jungle. It was only a matter of time before I bumped into one. They were on the hill above me. There might be more down here. I pressed on, often glancing uphill, expecting the cavalry to charge at every moment. There was no bog to run to here. No escape.

At last, I reached the top of the hill and the final hurdle: a shoulder-high drystone wall. More like a wet and slippery stone wall by now, but I found a way across and held out my hand to touch the tor. Shipley Tor. I'd made it. A lovely tor, actually, for all the pain. It was a good sort of shape with what I imagined would be a great view if half of it hadn't been taken out by fog.

I sat on Shipley Tor, but not for long. It was coming up to 3 o'clock and I still had two more tors to tick off – albeit with a good six kilometres between them. The day wasn't over yet.

Now the nightmare of Shipley was over, I started to

dream of the yellow brick road into camp. The well paved motorway of a track: the Two Moors Way. People call it the Puff 'n' Billy because it used to be the railway line from Ivybridge into Red Lake, an old china clay works built and abandoned in the early 1900s. If there's one thing great about a dismantled railway it's that whoever made it has gone out of their way to find the flattest route across the landscape. It looked so inviting on the map, a great big dotted line to tear along.

Stumbling back down through the undergrowth from Shipley Tor, I made it to the tarmac then up again, scrambling through the trees and rhododendrons on the other side of the river. Beyond them, I reached Black Tor. My second Black Tor of the walk. Two down, one to go. The rain was relentless, but I was back on open moorland now. Embracing the bog, I plodded onwards and thought of the Two Moors Way. Soon I'd be able to just get my head down and walk. Relax. Turn my brain off.

Not long now, but I really wanted a path to get me there too. I found the dismantled tramway that was marked on the map. At least, I thought the faint line in the ground was probably a dismantled tramway. It was in about the right place and going in the right sort of direction. But it wasn't really a path. The bog here was intense: just a shallow layer of moss and grass keeping you out of the peat. The kind of bog that bubbles up into wobbling crust, like walking on a giant's stomach.

There is an old Dartmoor story about a man who spots a top hat in the bog while he's out walking. The man is pleasantly surprised by his discovery and picks his way through the bog to retrieve it. But, upon lifting up the hat, he finds something even more surprising. Looking up out of the bog is a face: the hat's owner. The astonished walker offers to go and get some help to pull the man out of the bog. The man agrees – but only on the condition that the horse he is riding is pulled out too! Seems far-fetched, but right then I could believe it.

Some way along the thing that was probably once a tramway, I came across a boundary stone. It was about waist high and the width of a railway sleeper. I couldn't see any markings. Wiping the water off my map, I looked for the boundary stone. BS: there it was. According to the map I was going parallel to the Two Moors Way. I could carry on for a kilometre until the two paths joined, or I could walk 100 metres off piste and be on the dream path.

I looked to my left. The fog had lifted slightly, but I still couldn't see 100 metres. What I could see was heather, brash and bog. I looked back at the map. I couldn't wait. I turned and stepped into the heather.

At pace number 53, I stumbled out of the heather and into a ditch. Clambering across the ditch, I saw it: the promised land. I hurried over to meet it.

The Two Moors Way was no longer a bridleway. It was the Two Moors River. The moor was saturated and water knows what's best for it. It'll always find the easiest way off the hill. In this case, it had beaten me to it. The beautiful, flat, sand coloured path was flowing a couple of inches deep. My feet were already soaked. I needed this path. I stepped in.

At some points the water pooled into sections higher than my boots. It was too difficult to walk around the edges, so I just ploughed on through. This would have been alright if my gaiters actually worked. I'd slashed them open with a pair of crampons years ago and never quite got around to fixing them. They had far too much sentimental value to be replaced. I'd had them since my first Ten Tors walk, when their main function was to keep my you'll-grow-into-them trousers from dragging on the floor. Now that they didn't even perform their basic function of keeping my feet dry, you could say that they were essentially a fashion item. And since shorts and gaiters is the hottest look on Dartmoor, I suppose they probably were. Not that it was the right weather for shorts.

A voice in the back of my head told me I needed to eat something. It had been a while since I'd had some decent food, but I didn't want to stop. Instead, I pulled out a handy bag of Sports Mix from my pocket. Plodder lore tells us that each colour sweet has a different medicinal property: red for uphill, orange for blisters – or was it yellow? I couldn't remember. All I knew was that you could only eat the black ones if they'd been left on a trig point in the rain for at least an hour. Of course, we tried. Only later did I find out it was meant to make us leave them in the packet. They were Stu's favourite flavour. Pouring a handful into my oversized glove, I stuffed them into my mouth unscrupulously. One of them should work.

It was hard to chew and breathe at the same time. But I couldn't slow down. It was too wet. I'd get too cold. I just needed to power through. The rain ran down my face and soaked slowly into my inside layers. I just accepted it. There was nothing I could do to make it better. I just needed to get it over with as quickly as possible.

On my Mountain Leader Training course, they'd talked about the Five Ps of Engagement. As I walked, I could feel myself slipping from Participant into Passenger, starting to lose control of the situation. It felt a bit like falling asleep. The machine keeps moving but your brain drifts into moments of half-dream. You're no longer quite there any more. You try to focus, but it requires physical effort to wrestle yourself away from the cozy daze of dreaming, back to here and now.

More sugar. Keep moving. I was starving. Had I eaten lunch? The wind picked up as I crested the last corner before Sharp Tor. I'd need to get out of the river soon. Come on brain, hang on in there. We're going to get there. I observed as my body did indeed take a turning off the Two Moors Way and clamber over to the rock stack on the edge of Sharp Tor. We'd made it.

The freezing force of the wind brought my mind back into my body in a state of earnest. I'd stopped. I was getting cold. It was getting dark. I was running out of time. This was becoming dangerous. I needed to get a tent up, right now. Perhaps there was somewhere below the tor I could pitch? No, too many rocks. How about tucked behind the wall?

It was too slow, too late. I just needed somewhere – anywhere. I was almost out of wall. The wind was so cold. There was a lumpy patch in front of me with a clump of reed that could probably end up in the porch. I went for it. That'll do.

I threw up my tent as close to the wall as possible. The tent pegs barely went in, but I managed to tie a guy rope to the wall. Crouched in the porch, I stripped off all my wet layers and crawled into the tent. The tent was still wet from last night. Hurriedly, I got into the only dry things I had left: socks, thermal leggings and a Dartmoor Rescue t-shirt. Trying to keep these new clothes dry, I inflated my mat and unfurled my sleeping bag. It was down-filled. It was damp. I put a hat back on, pulled the sleeping bag hood tight around my face and lay still. I shivered.

After a little while, I felt warm enough to put the hood down. I wasn't producing enough body heat to really warm up the bag, so I pulled on the least damp fleece, hoping that was the right decision. If only I'd brought more spare layers instead of 10 bags of porridge. I sorted out my wet kit by torchlight, wringing or shaking it out and moving it to somewhere drier than the tent porch. Then I ate some food, wondering if I should have brought even a couple of wet ration packs, just so I could eat them cold. Boiling water was beyond me at the moment.

Everything done, I settled back down into my sleeping bag for the night. Heck, that was close. Was I warm enough to fall asleep? It's dangerous falling asleep when you're cold. You might not wake up. But that, sensible thoughts told panicking thoughts, is only when you're very cold. You're not that cold. You're okay now.

I lay still, listening to the rain slap against the tent and watching the fabric shake in the gusts. Oh the irony of getting hypothermic in a Dartmoor Rescue t-shirt. If I died overnight and someone found me like this, I'd have to die all over again of embarrassment.

CHAPTER 17 – HOME

The light woke me up. I rolled over in a confused daze. What happened to my alarm? What time was it? I reached over to the tent pocket and pulled out my watch. The screen was dark. I pressed the button for light. Nothing. I sat up and grabbed a head torch to get a better look. The screen was completely blank, with steamy droplets on the wrong side of the glass. Time had left us.

Without any idea of how late I was running, I got up and got going. Having to wear a complete set of wet clothes only added to my haste. It wasn't raining, but there were towering black clouds in the distance and wind enough to bring them over.

"If it rains like that again today," I thought, "then I might have to bin it."

I was 24 tors and less than 48 hours away from the finish. But if I didn't get a chance to dry out, I'd have to abandon the challenge. It was too dangerous.

Against all odds, the weather cleared. There wasn't much left to do. All I needed was to close this loop and get back into the main bit of the moor below Princetown. I kept walking.

A passer-by spotted me brushing my teeth in a country lane, wearing full waterproofs. I hadn't intended to be there, but I was still suffering from navigational exhaustion. I had taken the wrong road and ignored all the evidence telling me to turn back. When questioning the correctness of a road sign, know that it most certainly goes where it says it does.

As the morning passed, I picked off a couple of the most southerly tors with long walks in between them. I found a way around the modern China Clay Works and felt like a proper survivalist for successfully digging a toilet hole in the woods, before promptly cutting my hand open on the trowel. Step aside Bear Grylls, I've got this.

I reached the day-tripping mecca of Cadover Bridge just after lunchtime, judging by the angle of the sun. It was windy but clear, so the car park was packed with vehicles. There was an icecream van. Picnic mats and hampers adorned the riverside as families had a relaxing afternoon's outing. Children played by the river while parents read or chatted. I observed them like they were part of another world.

I was a Dartmoor thing. Socks full of Dartmoor bog, hair washed in Dartmoor rain – and I didn't care. While pristine people got out of their shiny cars and sat on folding camping chairs, I wallowed in my filth. Plonking my bag down, I lay back on the grassy bank as if it was a sofa. It was sunny. I could see. What more could a girl want?

After a few moments' sunbathing, I retrieved yesterday's socks from somewhere at the bottom of my rucksack. Wringing out as much brown water as I could onto the grass beside me, I tied them on the outside of my rucksack to dry. Satisfied with my washing line, I carried on up the track to Trowlesworthy.

Tor number 100. I lay down on the rocks below Great Trowlesworthy Tor, out of the wind. It was warm and you could see all the way out to Plymouth Sound and the sea. I'd kind of expected to be dancing around and excited by this point in the journey. But actually, I didn't know how I felt. Certainly not like dancing. Quietly lost in thought, I gazed out at the blue horizon.

There were only a few more tors left for today and lots of sun left in the sky. I ambled across the hillside, without a care in the world. I was home. Everywhere I walked and everywhere I looked reminded me of something. As I walked across the moor, I was walking through layers of memories. Some were dark and miserable nights, others bright successful days – and everything in between. This is where we sat on Bronze DofE because we weren't allowed to be ahead of our route card. Here is the path we used to take on Sunday morning reps between Trowlesworthy and Higher Hartor.

Memories came to me as I walked, unbidden, like I was experiencing the world with an extra dimension on top:

time. I couldn't tell you what it was like on that hillside that day, because I wasn't there. I was dancing down the slope in a bunch of teenage girls. I was standing in the dark being told "about a kilometre" was simply not accurate enough. I was chatting nonsense and university applications with my Ten Tors friends. I was waking up at 4:30 am to icy cold mornings, melting my shoelaces and wishing I'd kept the gas in the tent. They were everywhere and I walked through them.

It's a good job I knew where I was going. My waterproof Laminated Tough Map was sodden. The plastic was coming away from the paper, creating an extensive case of double vision. It was impossible to read, never mind take a bearing off. But in this weather I didn't need a map. This was my back garden and I'd walked every inch of it over more than half my life.

Before too long, I'd ticked off my tor quota with plenty of time left to camp. I knew just the place. We often used it with the Plodders. Soon I was sitting on the familiar grass, everything exactly like it always was. It wasn't anything particularly special, but it felt safe and homely. There were so many memories here.

In fact, I'd camped here for my 18th birthday party. A few friends and I had walked out to the spot, expecting to have the place to ourselves for the night. But we'd arrived to find tents already pitched. It was Stu and his DofE group. I always told him he'd crashed my 18th birthday party.

In classic Stu fashion, he rustled me up some birthday presents at a moment's notice. He gave me a pack of cards, a metal camping fork – presented with ceremony as the 'Fork of Fortitude' – and a chocolate pudding ration pack from the year I was born. Where exactly he'd found that ration pack, I hate to think.

Stu would have loved this mad idea of mine. Walking all the tors? Hardcore. Bonkers. Excellent. While other people might offer caution or concern, he would have just given me an enormous grin and told me to get on with it. But he'll never know. I wish I could tell him that I'm in Dartmoor Rescue now and that I'm a Mountain Leader too. I wish I could tell him that that little girl who fell into the leat on her first night navigation exercise is now helping to pinpoint casualties at 3 o'clock in the morning. I stared at the grass, wishing I could tell him that I'd almost been to every tor on Dartmoor in one go.

Stu died of cancer while I was at university. He'd had a diagnosis a few years before and recovered. This time, I didn't even know he was in hospital. The first thing I knew about it was being added to a group chat of over a hundred people. I thought it was spam. Nope: legions of Plodders. Then Huck rang me on Stu's phone to tell me the news and I half expected Stu to answer, laughing that he'd fooled us, acknowledging that it had got a little out of hand. He was exactly the kind of person to fake his own death for a cheap laugh and have enough charisma to get away with it. But it wasn't him. It was real.

He's not here. But there I was, sitting on the grass, transported to some other time entirely when he was here, right here, and so was I. The memories were as fresh as yesterday. I leant back against the big rock, thinking through the past week of walking. He's not here and yet he is here.

In fact, they were all here. Everyone I'd deliberately left behind to go on this adventure had come with me. They were echoes and memories, tied to the land, distant voices, each accompanied by a past version of me. Wherever I went I would see them, whenever I came back they would be there. I couldn't escape them because they make Dartmoor what it is to me. Untangle the people from the moors, the experiences from the place and I'd be left with an empty landscape. I'd still love it, but not so deeply. Not in the same way.

And perhaps that's what belonging to a place really means. You're not just seeing it on the surface, but through years and years of shared experience. You see through the veneer of the present into layers and layers of varnish, the actual object buried far underneath. Every layer has meaning and memories. To belong is to have a deep connection with a place, a shared history. I didn't have always, but I had enough.

I walked over to the only flat spot, the place no one else was ever allowed to camp on – even if they arrived first.

"I hope you don't mind me camping in your spot tonight," I said to the grass.

The tent pitched perfectly. I settled down behind the rock, stove bubbling, snuggled in a warm jacket. The sunset cast a golden light over the familiar landscape. Reaching into my bag, I cracked off a row of Steve's chocolate.

CHAPTER 18 – FERAL

Crouching down by the river below Black Tor, I scooped up some water into my Camelbak. It wasn't ideal for drinking water, but I didn't have a lot of options – and I certainly wasn't going to take it from the leat. The day had started with frost on my tent, but within hours, the icy glaze melted into a blue sky day. The way was straightforward. I knew where I was and where I was going. I'd walked these routes so many times before.

As I screwed the top back onto my Camelbak, a dog bounded down the slope towards me and sploshed about in the river. I looked back at my water, dubiously.

By the time I had my rucksack back on, the dog's owners had reached the river too. They looked me up and down.

"Are you the young lady from the front of the Tavi Times?"

"They put me on the front page did they!"

"Well," he considered, "on one of the pages."

"I'm doing all the tors in one go. Black Tor's number 114."

"That's it. I thought it would be you when I saw the size of your rucksack."

I smiled. It was the same size as every Ten Tors kid had ever hauled across Dartmoor and by now it was almost empty.

"How have you been getting on?" asked the lady.

"Weather's been pretty miserable, but I'm nearly done now. Only a handful of tors to go."

It had been a strange day. Now that the end was in sight and the weather mild, I'd completely lost motivation. Not because I didn't want to finish. Quite the opposite. As I left my campsite, I'd realised I could be finished by lunchtime. But I couldn't. Over the past few days, I'd been in touch with Andy, sporadically via text, trying to arrange for the press to come to the finish. They'd needed a time. I'd said 10 am tomorrow. The time was set and I was stuck.

I left the couple and ambled up to Black Tor. There was no hurry, I had so much time to kill. Heading straight up the steep side, I soon reached the top and passed its rocky stack. Should I wait here for a bit? There were only two more tors left on the day's list. I stood and took in the view for a moment: where I'd come from, via the whole of Dartmoor, and where I was going. The familiar clump of trees on the horizon marking just how close to the finish line I was.

Crossing the road behind Black Tor, I started to walk up Leeden Tor. Someone was waiting for me at the top. I gave a cautious wave and they waved back. It was Mark.

"Yay, you found me! Sorry I didn't make it last time."

"Much better weather for hanging around in this time," said Mark. "I've brought you a spare phone for the radio interview tomorrow. You can just put your SIM in it and they'll ring you like normal."

The press had been harassing Andy, who seemed to have turned into my PR guy, for a radio interview with me tomorrow morning before the finish. Frankly, I would have rather had a lie in. I'd been fending them off by saying, truthfully, that I had low phone battery. But they were really keen. Eventually I agreed.

"And there I was thinking you'd come to see me," I said softly.

I'd meant it with a hint of sarcasm but it felt wrong as soon as the words came out my mouth. This was the guy who'd spent two hours on Higher White Tor waiting for me.

Mark didn't seem to hear and was already heading down Leeden Tor towards his car. I walked with him.

"They've said to have a think about the sort of things they might ask you," he continued. "You know, like how the weather's been, what was the most difficult part – or the best and worst bits."

"Okay, I think I can manage that..."

We were passing through a herd of cows. I spun around in alarm. Mark walked straight through the middle, blithely unaware of my panic and still talking. I hurried after him.

"... they are going to send a TV crew out tomorrow morning to see you..."

At least there was someone to get my back if they all attacked at once.

"... are you excited to finish?"

"Um, I don't know really," I said, looking back over my shoulder at the cows. "It's odd. I'm definitely ready to finish. It's just that it's so close, but I have to wait until tomorrow to actually do it."

"You could just knock it off now, go home, have dinner and come back out in time for the finish tomorrow," said Mark, as if it was the most normal thing in the world.

I thought about it. From here I could walk home in two hours. The remaining handful of tors would take, what, an hour and a half max? I could finish now and be home in time for dinner.

"You're right. I could."

Yet it didn't feel right somehow. All the effort that had gone into organising the finish, all the people who'd got behind this walk. I didn't want to cheat them. This wasn't just about me any more.

"I told everyone 10 am tomorrow," I said finally. "It wouldn't be right to finish earlier."

"Okay," he said. "Well, you'll be needing this then."

He handed me the spare phone and we checked that it accepted my SIM card. As we stood in the car park, a Dartmoor Ranger drove past in his Land Rover. He stopped to roll down the window and wave.

"Well done!" he exclaimed and, after a brief and cheery chat, drove off again.

"Do you know him?" I asked Mark.

"I don't think so..."

"Maybe he's just friendly with everyone."

"Nah, this is your five minutes of fame."

Mark left me to slowly collect my last tor of the day. I sat on Leather Tor for as long as I could manage. One hundred and sixteen tors down, three more to go, but none today. Eventually, I thought I may as well go and find a nice camping spot. I walked down the hill and back into the area I was allowed to camp. Even at beyond the prescribed 100 metres from the road, it still felt way too public.

I chose a spot and sat down on the grass. It was 4 o'clock.

"Hmm," I thought. "Now what?"

I wasn't really hungry, but I supposed I may as well cook dinner, for something else to do. I'd almost reached the end of my food. At lunchtime I had eaten my final peanut butter wrap, slowly, wistfully, imagining I might never have occasion to eat one again. It's not the sort of thing you eat in normal life, but I'd grown rather fond.

My stove boiled. A 900 kcal vegetable curry and the rest of Steve's chocolate later, I paused.

"Maybe I am hungry."

But I couldn't eat everything now and have none left for tomorrow.

Several hours later, I was still in exactly the same spot when Andy arrived, dressed like he'd come straight from work. He took a waterproof jacket out his bag, placed it open on the ground beside me and sat on it. I felt feral.

"How are you doing?"

"Well!"

We talked about how the walk had gone, what it had been like to be out on my own on the moors for so long.

Then conversation turned to the finish. Andy started to run me through the logistics.

"You're going to have a TV crew come out to meet you at Princetown. We've got permission to set up the Team gazebo in the square and a 50th Anniversary banner. We should get a good turn out from the Team. I'm just trying to find the right person to ask for permission to park a Team vehicle on the square, to have a bit more of a presence."

"Oh, I can put you in touch with Mike. He'd know."

"That would be really helpful, thanks. So all that and then the radio interview in the morning. You're all set for that now, right?"

"Yes, it's all sorted."

"Paul says he's going to come out and see you in the morning."

"Oh, why? Mark gave me a phone earlier – he knows right?"

Paul is our Team Leader, the one in charge of operations, who sits on all the committees and deals directly with the other Emergency Services. He's been in Dartmoor Rescue for over 25 years and knows the moor backwards. There had been talk of Paul coming out to lend me his phone and have the press ring that instead.

Andy smiled, "I think there's a part of Paul that wants to come and see you out here, like this, before it's all over."

Briefing for the finish completed and daylight fading, Andy had to head off back home.

"Thanks so much for organising all this, Andy."

"No problem. I only wish I could be there myself to see it all."

He took a quick couple of photos of me setting up my tent in the sunset, for social media, and headed home. The sun set on the All the Tors Challenge.

CHAPTER 19 – FINISHED

"Are you awake in there?" called a familiar voice.

"Yes," I chorused and scrambled to undo the tent zips to prove it. It was Paul.

"Having a lie in are we?"

"Well if I have to do this interview I'm certainly not getting out of my sleeping bag for it!"

The sun was still rising. Paul sat on the grass bank beside my tent.

"Have you got everything you need?"

I waved Mark's phone, "All set. They said they'd ring me just before half seven."

"Well, I brought you something."

He threw a bag of jelly babies across the pile of kit in the porch. I leant over to reach it and grinned. I had no idea my jelly baby vibe was so strong.

"Thank you."

"Probably not to eat for breakfast."

The phone rang and I retreated back inside the tent. Somehow, sitting in a tent made the whole radio interview experience feel less serious.

"Where are you calling us from Emily?" asked the radio host in a loud, jovial voice.

"I'm in a tent, just south of Princetown..."

After 15 minutes of light-hearted banter, I signed off with my fundraising link and waited to hear the crackling voice of the guy who brought me on come back into my ear. No one did, it was just the radio, so I hung up. We'd had a nice little chat about the walk, hopefully enough for people to get the gist. Although I had been repeatedly pressed for my opinions on Doctor Who. Maybe all radio interviews are just strange.

"All done?" asked Paul as I popped my head back out the porch.

"Yep – so much better than last time. I'd better start packing this tent up, it's getting late."

"Right. Well, I'll drive round to Princetown and help them set up. The TV crew said they'd be arriving early. You still on target for 10 o'clock?"

"What time is it?"

"Coming up to eight."

"Yeah, easy."

"Okay, well keep in touch so I can manage the press."

"Okay. I'll ring you at the last tor."

"Great. See you on the other side."

He left and I quickly packed up my tent for the last time.

My rucksack was almost empty now, camping equipment rolling about in all the space as I walked. I slipped open the packet of jelly babies and ate a couple. My food was almost completely eaten, but it didn't matter now. Within hours I could be sitting in a kitchen or a cafe with my feet up, eating whatever I wanted. I could hold on.

It was almost too easy: a perfect path all the way to the finish. I loped along in the golden morning, cutting off the path here and there to collect the remaining few tors. Before I knew it, I was standing on King's Tor. Tor number 119. The last.

I grabbed the camera and spun around in circles with it laughing, shouting, "All the tors!"

All the flipping tors. It was done.

My phone rang.

"Hi Paul."

"Just ringing to see where you're at."

"I'm on top of King's Tor. My last tor." I added.

"So that's it, you're finished? There isn't anywhere else you need to go?"

"There is nowhere else I need to go," I said. "I'm coming home."

I started to walk down the hill when my phone rang again, "Hello?"

"Sorry to bother you, Emily. The press have decided that they want to come out and meet you actually on the moors, before you get back into Princetown. They're not really dressed for it, so I'm not letting them go off the dismantled railway line. Don't want any unexpected casualties. One of them's in trainers and carrying a huge camera round with her."

"Yeah, that would be embarrassing..."

"So we'll meet you on the railway line then, you know by the bridge before the gate? Give them some nice views of the moor."

"I know it."

"Good. You'd better get your make-up on," he quipped, "they've brought an enormous camera."

"Sure," I laughed. I'd never put make-up on in my life and he knew it. "I think I'd better put a hat on."

As I rounded the final bend of the railway track, a small group of people was waiting to meet me. Paul was there and three or four Dartmoor Rescue teammates, including one trainee, ecstatic to have been lent a red jacket for their part in the show. The TV presenter, Naomi, introduced herself and her camerawoman Molly, a small athletic-looking lady in leggings, hulking a camera half her size around on one shoulder. It was the biggest camera I'd ever seen.

We walked up and down the railway line, back and forth, getting different shots. They even strapped a GoPro to my head for one take. Naomi walked beside me and asked me basic, friendly questions about the walk.

"What are you most looking forward to when you're finished?"

"A hot shower, a warm fire and a sofa. Probably in that order."

Then we'd do it all again, pretending to talk, while Molly got a long shot from the hillside.

I could see Paul getting impatient as the takes dragged on and on.

"You're going to have to let this young lady go," he said eventually. "She said she'd be back in Princetown by 10 and it's already just past. There are people waiting for her. Perhaps you go on ahead so you can get a shot of her finishing?"

Naomi agreed and hurried off with a few others.

"I just want to get a shot of the sheep!" called Molly after her.

I walked slowly down the track with Paul, behind everyone, until they were out of sight.

He winked, "I had to say something or we'd have been stuck up here all day. They would have never let you finish!" He held the final gate open, "Off you go."

I stepped through the gate and started to run. It is a Dartmoor Plodders tradition to run through Princetown. Partly for the home sprint into the Fox Tor Cafe, partly so other people will look up and take notice.

"Who's that?" A passer-by will ask their friends.

"Oh," someone else will answer, "that's the Dartmoor Plodders."

I charged down the hill into Princetown, clattering down the road, feet slapping on the tarmac. Past the fire station, past the brewery, I'd forgotten just how far a sprint it was on exhausted legs. I reached the car park and cut across. My sore, wrinkly feet pounded onwards, the contents of my rucksack shook and bounced about behind me. I slowed to a shuffle on the uphill. Nearly there, one last push. I turned the corner. The Visitor Centre came into view – and the square, filled with a sea of red. They started cheering.

I tumbled downhill into the square and stopped amid a crowd of smiling people. It was over.

"I made it."

I'd crossed the finish line. The crowd surrounded me.

I was amazed at how many people had come to see me in. Some were friends, some trainees who I barely knew at all yet, and many inbetween. My parents, of course, were in the crowd, as were some Dartmoor National Park staff and a few Princetown residents who'd got interested. It felt a bit like a fundraising event. In fact, it would be easy to be cynical and say they were only there to put on a good show for the camera. But I knew deep down that wasn't true. You could have got away with half as many people. They were here for me.

The TV crew had actually missed my triumphant return into Princetown, trying to move their van out of the shot. So instead they lined us all up in front of the Team gazebo, with me front and centre, while Mike from Dartmoor National Park took a photo. They were filming him do it, so it very quickly felt very staged. We were all left standing under the gazebo, grinning awkwardly and wondering if we were allowed to move yet. I turned around to look at everyone but was at a loss for what to say. Then someone at the back piped up, "Oy, what time to do call this? You're late!"

We all burst out laughing.

I ditched the rucksack and went over to hug Mum and Dad. Then Mark and some others came in for a hug too or to pass on congratulations. Someone handed me a flask of hot chocolate with a conspiratorial whisper, "It's from the Fox Tor Cafe and they say there's another one behind the counter for you whenever you want it."

The rest of the morning passed in a daze. Mum was liberally handing out cupcakes to anyone who didn't refuse hard enough. Dad was making friends with Search Dog Jess. I did interview after interview, for the TV, for the radio – for who knows what! Paul did one too about the Team and our 50th. A local cafe came and decked us out with hot drinks. There were banners and balloons – the latter a little Dartmoor Rescue in-joke, a nod to the time I impulsively ran across Duck's Pool chasing a helium balloon.

It felt like I'd organised a party. As people started to disperse, I said the goodbyes like any good host, "Thank you! Thank you so much for coming!"

Yet at the same time I was very aware that none of this party was my doing. It had been arranged around me, for me, by others, some who couldn't even be here for it. I guess it was like a surprise party. I'd never had one of those before, but I liked it.

As the last people were leaving and the gazebo was being packed away, I walked back over to the car with my parents. It was over and I could barely process it. Easing my bag down into the boot of the car, I stopped for more photos from Mum. I held a gold 'Welcome Home' balloon in each hand.

"Well," I said, sitting down, "I don't suppose you brought any flip flops...?"

EPILOGUE

The All the Tors Challenge finished up very much like a normal Ten Tors. When we got home, I emptied my bag out onto the lawn, leaving its contents to dry in the sun. I spread out the map and the tent, safe in the knowledge that nothing was going to blow them away – and it didn't even matter if they did because I was sleeping in a house tonight. My socks were soaked in a bucket before they were allowed near the washing machine. They turned the water black (a number of times). What little rubbish I had went in the bin and I clipped the cable ties off the laminated sign that had been attached to my bag the entire walk. It was fairly worse for wear, the paper sheet inside no longer entirely dry, but it now read 119/119 in proud red letters.

Having my first hot shower in 10 days felt as luxurious as I'd imagined it. Although I did lose an entire layer of skin off the bottom of each foot. All those hard won calluses, from years of walking, simply peeled off. Each time I showered, I had to check I hadn't left the soles of my feet behind.

My life slowly went back to normal. Or at least a normal that didn't involve walking a long way, eating dehydrated food and sleeping in a tent. I would like to say that I enjoyed being indoors while it rained outside, but the weather was gloriously sunny for the rest of the month. I was back at work the very next day – because you use a laptop with your hands not your feet. But the phone kept ringing and emails kept coming in with requests for articles and interviews. For about a week I felt like a celebrity. If I went into town, I'd smile at everyone, just in case they recognised me.

I thought it was just my five minutes of fame and to some extent it was. Very quickly, the news moved on and the phone stopped ringing. But something strange happened. Weeks, even months later, people would come up to me, strangers at local events or friends' parties. People I'd never met or seen before.

"You look familiar," they'd say.

Or perhaps, "I saw you on TV!"

In fact, at my work's Christmas party, more people exclaimed that they'd seen me on TV than wished me a Happy Christmas.

Of course, it wasn't all good. There were a few people who were quick to point out that someone else had probably visited all these tors already. I mean, that wasn't the point but whatever. One particularly outraged resident of the East Moor declared that he may as well draw a ring around the Haytor area, call it Dartmoor and do All the Tors in a single day. But generally, people were positive.

The Ten Tors season started again, as it always does. I was back out on the moors again almost without a break, trailing behind groups of teenagers or sitting on tors and in cafes. Well, one cafe in particular. The Plodders had lots of questions about the walk. Specific, practical questions from people who are building up their own encyclopedic knowledge of Dartmoor. Which route did you take between these two tors? How did you find being alone for so long? What were your blisters like? How did you sort out the food? They couldn't believe I'd got everything into a 60 litre bag, like the ones on their backs. It made it almost seem possible.

In fact, it was only when talking through my Bench-Shipley ordeal with the 45s, that I started to doubt the cow. Looking back on it, I no longer have any idea if that cow was real. It seemed very real at the time and I was genuinely mistaking gorse bushes for cows at the edge of the fog. But this cow appeared out of thin air. It was not there. Then, suddenly, it was.

The brain can do strange things when we're really tired. I've seen things once before: huge bugs crawling through long grass at the edge of my torch light in the small hours of the morning. But they were shadowy and indistinct compared to this cow. Perhaps it did sneak up on me and I was too absorbed in the map to hear it. But I'll never really know and I find that somewhat unsettling.

As for cows in general, sleep and company when out walking has abated that paranoia. I no longer think that they are all out to get me. But I certainly don't trust them and would much rather avoid them at all costs – especially in the summer and especially in the fog.

And in case there is any shadow of a doubt, no I haven't been put off Dartmoor or multi-day solo expeditions. I've been asked many times if I would do it all again and the answer is: perhaps, but not in a hurry. I am very glad I did it, but it's not something I want to repeat for quite a while.

But even so, something strange has happened between me and All the Tors. I can't escape it, it's part of me now. We're connected like the word association game. Perhaps that's partly why I wanted to write this book. I thought it would have worn off by now, but it hasn't. The All the Tors Challenge is just another layer of Dartmoor history. That's not why I did the walk, as you know. I didn't think it would be something other people remembered or even noticed. But I'm flattered to have a tiny part in the long heritage of walking on Dartmoor.

Years on, local people still sidle up to me with varying degrees of conviction and ask the same eight words.

"Are you that girl who did that walk?"

"Yes," I say, "yes I am."

AUTHOR'S NOTES

Oh, so you're still reading are you? Don't worry, I do that too while the book sinks in. You have no obligation to read this bit, but I've got some good news for you if you do.

First though, while I have your attention, could you do me a favour? Stop right here, right now and leave a review on whatever platform you bought this book from. If you borrowed it off a friend, rescued it from a Dartmoor bog or found it under a rock in the Atacama Desert then I'm still talking to you. Amazon is probably your best bet for placing thoughts. Even if it's a single sentence, your words really help future readers. I'll wait right here while you go and do it.

Done? Great – thank you! Now here's the good news: if you liked this book, which I hope you did since you're still here, there's a lot more of my writing floating around the ether. You can find hundreds of articles on my website where I write about adventure, writing, Dartmoor (of course) and roughly anything else that pops into my head. Want to know more about me, what I'm up to now and what's coming next? Then definitely check out that website. It'll have all the most up to date information. Take a browse at travellinglines.com

Second piece of news: I'm a real person. Which means that, if you'd like to chat with me via the internet you can. I'm @travellingline on Twitter and @travellinglines everywhere else. I have an endless capacity for sharing the love of Dartmoor: fog, bog and tors, send them all my way. If you have specific adventure or book related questions, I'll do my best to help you. There's also a contact form on my website. If all else fails, send me a pigeon. I'll leave the window open.

SOME THANK YOUS

Thanking people is a dangerous business. Once you start a list, you're always at risk of missing someone out. I'm going to try to keep this succinct and broad, but if you're in this group, you'll know who you are.

To my characters, thank you for letting me include you in this book. It would be very bland without you. The people in these pages are only shadows and footprints of the real people involved. Even the most well-rounded character is still only the impression of a person. Real people are far more complicated. It goes without saying that everything herein is a version of the world seen through my eyes and the lens of story.

To everyone who helped make the All the Tors Challenge itself happen. Even (especially) if you didn't make it into the book. A particular mention should go to SPOT, Vaude, Firepot and the Next Challenge Grant for their support.

To my Mum and Dad, for warming to the idea that long and isolated expeditions are what their daughter calls fun and that she'll be off on many more in the future. Thank you for everything.

To the people who helped to turn this book into a reality. In particular, Alex Stoecker for ensuring that I left the house and Anna McNuff for being extremely enthusiastic and helpful at just the moment I was starting to get nervous.

To you, my Adventure Squad. It still baffles me how many people read my writing and support my adventures. Thank you for making it all the more fun. If this is the first thing of mine you've read, welcome! I'd love to have you along for the ride.

ON DARTMOOR RESCUE

There are actually four independent Mountain Rescue teams that cover Dartmoor from north, south, east and west. They are Dartmoor Search and Rescue Team Okehampton, Plymouth, Ashburton and Tavistock respectively. That's a bit of a mouthful, so I hope you'll forgive me for contracting to simply Dartmoor Rescue.

ON DARTMOOR NERDS

As you may have guessed, I'm a bit of a Dartmoor Nerd myself. I hope that Grades Two and above can forgive me for poking fun at the pursuit. To my fellow Grade Ones, I wish you every happiness in mildly pursuing Dartmoor knowledge at your leisure. May your walks be ever enriched. To everyone else, if this book has even slightly whetted your appetite, I would highly recommend delving into the deep history and traditions of Dartmoor. Some good places to start would be Legendary Dartmoor's website, Dartmoor 365 or any number of books on the subject.

ON TEN TORS

When I did Ten Tors, it was just that: 10 actual tors and a 35, 45 or 55 mile route between them, measured as the crow flies. Although it has kept the name, by the time I did the All the Tors Challenge there had been a complete route overhaul. The new routes involve about 15 checkpoints, many of which are on the very edge of the moor, and rarely include as many as eight actual tors enroute. Given how contentious a topic tors are, as well you know from this book, it's surprising that this change seems to have gone completely unmarked. I hope that with all the advances in tracking and technology, the event will return to its former glory in the not too distant future.

YOUR TURN NEXT?

There will be a few of you who I haven't put off from the idea of visiting all the tors on Dartmoor. Some may even be considering recreating my route (I wish you better weather). For walkers who'd like to have a go at their own pace, logbooks are available from allthetorschallenge.com with a rucksack patch upon completion. Also, please consider this as me laying down the gauntlet. The route I took could be done in much less than 10 days with the right combination of weather and firing times. I would love to see you beat it – particularly if you are a Dartmoor Plodder.

CAMPING ON DARTMOOR

Dartmoor is one of the few places in the UK where it is still legal to wild camp. This is thanks to the Dartmoor Commons Act. However it is always worth remembering that the land which makes up Dartmoor is privately, not nationally, owned. We are able to camp by delicate agreement, not by right.

All walkers should follow Dartmoor National Park's Ranger Code. This is broadly common sense: be respectful of other users, take your litter home, don't feed the ponies (no matter how hard they coax you!), keep your dog on a lead and close gates behind you.

For camping, there is an up to date map available at dartmoor.gov.uk showing the exact boundaries of where it is acceptable to pitch. It is important to remember that this type of camping should only be done as I have in this book. You must be able to carry all your equipment in one rucksack, be sleeping out as part of your walk and move on each night. Your tent should be small (i.e. certainly not big enough to stand up in).

There is a lot more information available from the National Park, that can be found with a quick online search. I would highly encourage anyone thinking about visiting Dartmoor to do so. But the main points are about respect: don't light fires, don't leave anything behind (biodegradable or otherwise) and don't pitch too close to rivers or roads. Basically, unless someone passes you in the dark, no one should know that you've ever been there.

It's worth saying that there are a great many normal, comfortable, well equipped campsites on Dartmoor too. The range spans from empty field to all mod cons, so there will be something to suit most tastes. You will likely get a better night's sleep!

THE SUPPORTERS

Andy Barton
Sarah Williams
Martyn Jewell
Peter Rich
Kevin Winter
Sophie Johnstone
Matt Langsford
Rob Palmer
Rosie Sneyd
Katie Toghill
Alison Trigell
Mark Pinto
Elna Lerk – de Wolf
Paul Buck
Kate Wakelam
Charlotte B Birch
Richard Glanville
Leona Thorpe
Chris Bunney
Ruth Olley
Chris Sweetapple
Ellie Berry
Ali Cooper
Rachael Steel
Phae Leveridge
Rob McKenzie
Gill Borthwick
Venetia Lipscombe
Charlie
Lucy Evans
Max Piper
Kevin Bastow
Nadine Chant
Dockyard Venturers
John Hee
Peter Caton
Alison Owen
Tony Knight
Sam Clifford
Alan Pearn
Family Doets
Sandy P
Matt Daley
Bob Fitzpatrick
Matthew King
Jim Smith

John Flaherty
Simon Sorlie-Pring
Christopher Burridge-Barney
Nigel Machin
Graham Leonard Turner
Kenton Dalziel
David
Jules Ryder
Greg
Gail
Adam
Ulla-Maija Viitavuori
Daniel Davies-Llewellyn
Sir Twonkalot
Tom Brooks
Eric Berggren
Huccaby & Laura
Hannah Dart
Laura & Oliver Perratt
N.R. Jenzen-Jones
Jen Emeleus

My sincerest thanks for helping this book to see the light of day. I really hope you enjoyed reading it.

Lightning Source UK Ltd.
Milton Keynes UK
UKHW022141190522
403272UK00003B/101